THE PITMEN'S DERBY

THE PITMEN'S DERBY

A History of the Northumberland Plate

Mike Kirkup

MID NORTHUMBERLAND ARTS GROUP
1990

Published 1990 by
Mid Northumberland Arts Group
Leisure and Publicity Department
Town Hall, Ashington
Northumberland NE63 8RX

MidNAG is sponsored by Wansbeck District Council, and grant-aided by Northern Arts.

ACKNOWLEDGEMENTS
Grateful thanks to Newcastle City Library Local Studies; Newcastle Journal and Chronicle Photo and Archive Library; Northumberland Records Office; A C (Freddie) Newton; Doug Moscrop.

Other photographs from the Duke of Roxburghe, Jimmy Etherington, Ronnie Robson, Peter O'Sullevan, Palmer Photographic Newcastle, Jack Wallace, Reuben Daglish, David Parmley and High Gosforth Park Plc.

Caricatures courtesy *The Tout*;
Document caligraphy by Edna Ralph;
Painting front and back cover, 1882 Northumberland Plate by unknown artist;
Inside cover, painting by Tod Ramos of Trade Line, winner 1985, sponsored by Newcastle Breweries;
Illustrations by Phil Lockey.

ISBN 0 904790 69 X

Printed by Unit Offset Group

Contents

Cheers, for the Plate

Plate Day is not just about a field of thoroughbreds battling it out for supremacy over Gosforth Park's testing two miles. It's one of the great sporting and social highlights in the North-East.

An occasion for Tyneside folks to carry on with a family tradition – their fathers and grandfathers were always there for the Pitmen's Derby; an occasion when the womenfolk go out and treat themselves to a new attire, certainly a hat to wear on the big day; an occasion when the Hoppings come to the Town Moor, scene of the early days of the Plate when it was used as a racecourse and not as a vast amusement arcade. A far cry from Royal Ascot, but still a dress-conscious day; an occasion when Tyneside grabs the spotlight through the presence of the television cameras.

After all, the North-East has a lot to offer and is crying out for more recognition. Not long ago the Northumberland Plate was in danger of becoming just another handicap for stayers in the Racing Calendar. Attendances were on the decline and the meeting was losing its appeal, not only to Tyneside folk but to those outside the region who had once recognised the importance of such a day.

The race needed a financial injection and, despite the Jockey Club being rather shortsighted initially by not allowing handicaps to become more valuable than some prestigious conditions races, the Plate is now on terms with the best in the country. Thanks to Newcastle Breweries, the 1989 race was the richest ever with £50,000 added. Now we have a horserace that we can be proud of again. Provided the proposed developments at Gosforth Park are given the green light, the future of the sport in this superb setting will be assured.

If there's something in this world worth having, don't let us toss it away! And if racing at Newcastle is important to the area then it mustn't be allowed to become a big white elephant that only springs up once a year. Britain is still great! In sport, which other country could boast of having the Grand National; the Epsom Derby; and Wimbledon? Tradition, even on a local scale, doesn't materialise overnight and it is important that we support Gosforth Park, and so contribute to the continued success of the time-honoured Northumberland Plate.

Doug Moscrop *(Underhand of the Newcastle Journal)*

They're Off!

Now lads and lasses myed for toon,
An in the road they oft lay doon,
Faith! monny a lassie spoil'd her goon,
A Comin frae the Races, O.

Some gat hyem midst outs and ins,
Some had black eyes an broken shins,
An some lay drunk among the whins,
A Comin frae the Races, O.

It is clear from this old Geordie song that Newcastle Races enjoyed something of an alcoholic tradition from the very beginning. There has been horseracing of one kind or another in the North-East for the last 350 years. Initially, races were held at Killingworth on a stretch of moorland, and records indicate that the first meeting was in the early seventeeth century.

A scribe of 1610 recorded that Robert Delaval sent a letter to the Earl of Northumberland in which he referred to the 'colt that Sir John Fenwick gave the King that was held to be the swiftest horse in England, which was given to the Duke of Ulster'.

There is reference to the same John Fenwick in 1621, as being the man 'whose year it is to bring in the Plate'. The 'Plate' being the money collected as the prize for any particular race.

In 1632, twenty pounds was paid to John Blakiston Chamberlain by the Newcastle Corporation 'which he disbursed for two silver potts granted by the Common Council for the race on Killingworth Moor'. And in 1673 John Dodsworth in his last will and testament left 'my silver flagon which I won first at Killingworth Moor', to Thomas Gabetis.

Racing survived at Killingworth for almost 100 years until all races except the County Plate were transferred to Newcastle's Town Moor which became the City's official racing headquarters. The first meeting took place in 1721 and we need to wait only ten years before claims of drunken revelry through the entries in the diary of one Thomas Smales for June 1731:

June 12   To Newcastle Races. Very drunk.
June 13   Sunday. At do. Drinking day and night.
June 14   Won the Plate. Drinking day and night.
June 15   To Durham, soe to Aldbrough. Drinking all night.
June 16   To Gilling with Plates, so home very drunk.
June 17   At home very ill.
June 18   Do. Extream ill. In journey spent £15 17s 6d.

It seems that the racing on the Town Moor continued in the same outlandish manner with the 1738 programme containing an event for 'Asses to be rode by chimney sweeps, and their brushes to pay them along'. There was a half-guinea hat for the first man home in a footrace and a gown for ladies in a dancing display. Probably the forerunner of the 'make yourself sick' contest was 'supping hot, six bowls of Hasty Pudding and butter, the winner that sups most and soonest to receive a 2s 6d reward'.

Another favourite diversion at the races was cockfighting: the Geordie birds were champions! In his, *Sporting Tour through Northern Parts*, Colonel T Thornton reckoned 'Cockfighting is likely to flourish here more than in most parts of England ... this favourite amusement was everywhere the general topic of conversation'. Pierce Egan's *Book of Sports* estimated that at the end of any particular raceweek more than 1,000 cocks had crowed their last and that 'Newcastle may therefore challenge the world for cocking'.

If the goings-on at the Town Moor were rough and ready then the conditions for racing were even worse. Early facilities were described as 'in the most uncomfortable style imaginable ... there is no stand, unless an erection of coarse boards (which neither protects the company from wind nor weather, and where every squall endangers the necks of the occupiers) can be esteemed such'.

William Loftus, the first clerk of the course, remedied the deficiency by allowing that 'Silver tickets giving admission during the time of any race being run on the Town Moor be sold at 15 guineas to raise money for a grandstand'. That he was successful was verified by a visitor to the first meeting of the nineteenth century, when she wrote of the new stand: 'As convenient and commodious as could be wished, some say equal or better than at York. However, there was one incident which marred the pleasure when two gentlemen allowed some quarrel to heat their blood, and were like to settle the matter with their whips'.

Further improvements to the course were recorded in the *Newcastle Courant* of January 1822: 'A determination has been formed to alter the racecourse on the Town Moor of Newcastle-on-Tyne, according to suggestions of amateurs of the Turf, so as to avoid the hill on the west side'. As a result of the work carried out, the circuit was then measured as one mile, six furlongs and 132 yards round.

Racegoers at Newcastle in 1828 were taken aback when a seven-legged horse called Pincushion won two races. But when someone noticed that it was beginning to sprout an *eighth*, it was summarily despatched to the freak show at Cow Hill Fair.

Newcastle's principal race at the time was the Gold Cup, and a remarkable horse with the peculiar name of XYZ won it four times in a row. But it was still felt that not enough money was being put back into the sport and the *Sporting Magazine* noted 'Money and exertion, if liberally and judiciously used, would bring many of the best horses from the North of England and Scotland. Until this is the case Newcastle must content itself to be classed with the third-raters'. Twelve months later the same pamphlet noted 'We have been averted to the falling off of sport at Newcastle with regret not unmingled with hope of better things. The chief improvement in the list for the present year consists in the establishment of a handicap plate'. That year was 1833. The Northumberland Plate had begun!

First Winners of the Northumberland Plate Run on Town Moor

Date	Winner	Date	Winner
1833	Tomboy	1841	Calypso
1834	Fanny	1842	Heslington
1835	Satan	1843	Mosstrooper
1836	Cyprian	1844	The Era
1837	Wedge	1845	Inheritress
1838	St Bennet	1846	Dolo
1839	St Bennet	1847	Ervx
1840	Herman Platoff	1848	Chanticleer

Bee'swing, the Adopted Daughter of Northumberland

Some of the finest horses in the country competed for the new race. In 1836 a redoubtable animal called Cyprian pulled off an amazing feat of endurance by walking from the stable in Malton down to Epsom where she duly won the Oaks, then trudging all the way back again to take on and beat her three rivals in the Plate.

Caller Ou dual winner in 1863/4, had previously won the St Leger, beating the Derby winner Kettledrum in the process. Most successful owner of Plate winners was Mr R C Vyner, whose four winners ranged from Glastonbury in 1878 through to Killigrew in 1907. A name familiar to *Newcastle Journal* readers is Underhand, the Plate's only hat-trick specialist in 1857/8/9. But probably the most famous racehorse of all time *never* to win the Plate was the Northumbrian mare, Bee'swing.

> *Now I of Bee'swing sing, that gallant mare of fame,*
> *Go where she may, she beats them all*
> *And adds honour to her name.*
> *Her pedigree I will make known, if you the same require;*
> *I'll tell you what they called her dam,*
> *And what her noble sire.*
> *With all the Cups that she has won*
> *And purses filled with gold;*
> *Since in the Racing Calendar, Bee'swing has been enrolled.*
> *(Old North Country Ballad)*

Bee'swing, a bay mare, was foaled in 1833 the same year that its breeder Squire William Orde of Nunnykirk, Northumberland, entered and won the first-ever running Northumberland Plate on Newcastle's Town Moor with his horse Tomboy.

According to a pamphlet produced by M Benson, the Northumbrian mare became 'the admired of all admirers, the leading feature at all race meetings, the signal for one universal cheer from thousands of delighted spectators'. Although trained at Middleham she was, as Squire Orde later named her, *'The Adopted Daughter of Northumberland'.*

The performances of Bee'swing have rarely if ever been equalled. In these days where horseracing is a multi-million dollar sport, others have undoubtedly won a larger amount of money; others may have won more races, but Bee'swing was the unsurpassed character of her day.

Charles William Orde's land-owning family dates back to the early fourteenth century and a namesake was High Sheriff of Northumberland when Charles I was on the throne of England. A bachelor, he had been called to the Bar, but preferred the life of a country squire.

One of Orde's near neighbours, Ralph Riddell of Felton Park, owned a powerhouse of a horse called Doctor Syntax who picked up Gold Cups much the same way as other horses picked daisies.

In 1829 Orde bought an unnamed Ardrossan mare from Riddell and her foal that year was Plate winner Tomboy. The following year Orde and Riddell were having a glass of port together when news came to them of the birth of a Doctor Syntax filly. The men's drinking glasses were engraved with flying bees, 'Let's call her Bees'wing,' said Riddell raising his glass in a toast to the newcomer. 'I'll drink to that,' was Orde's reply, and a purple era had begun for Northumberland and its flying filly.

The Bees'wing colours of white, blue sleeves and cap, were entrusted to jockey John Cartwright by her trainer ex-Sunderland jockey Bob Johnson, who had stables at Tupgill, Middleham. She ran only three times as a two-year-old and was in fact well beaten on her first outing at Newcastle's Town Moor. Not a very auspicious beginning on a track that was to become her second home.

Next time out on September 14th at Doncaster, carrying 8st 3lbs, she won the five furlong Champagne Stakes in a race for 50 sovereigns, starting at the generous odds of 7–1, beating her five opponents according to the *Racing Calendar* 'very easily'. The following year she won the Newcastle St Leger over a mile and six furlongs starting second favourite at 7–4, beating the 6–5 favourite Black Diamond 'easily'.

Orde had built himself a reputation for being a heavy gambler and he embarked Bee'swing upon a career that sent her on a quest for 64 races, 51 of which saw the gallant mare in the winner's enclosure. Her one tilt at the Northumberland Plate was as a five-year-old in 1838, when an onerous 9st proved too much for the 4–6 favourite, and she was beaten into second place by Lord Eglington's St Bennet to whom she was trying to concede two stones. John Cartwright her jockey had to wait until 1850 before he rode a Northumberland Plate winner when Elthiron beat six opponents. He retired from racing soon afterwards and took himself a hostelry, The Ram Inn, but died at the age of 46 in 1860.

Squire Orde, probably unfairly, was considered a bit of an eccentric, and died shortly after Bee'swing's last victory, the Ascot Cup in 1842. The victim of an apoplectic fit, he collapsed in the gardens of The Queen's Head Hotel in Morpeth. He was succeeded by his nephew Charles William Orde who was not a racing man, but retained Bee'swing at stud until 1854 when she died in her twenty-first year.

At stud, Bee'swing's reputation was further enhanced by producing nine children or grandchildren to be Derby winners, eight Oaks winners, and 11 who succeeded in the Leger. For the following half a century her ancestors regeigned supreme. But it was her son Newminster, named after the old abbey in Morpeth, that was to prove so influential as a stallion in later years. The blood of Bee'swing changed the whole course of Turf history, and it is an interesting feature that no fewer than ten of Newminster's male progeny went on to win the Aintree Grand National.

Summary of Bee'swing's Performances

Years	Times of Starting	Won	Lost	Cups
1835	3	2	1	0
1836	5	2	3	1
1837	8	6	2	4
1838	9	7	2	3
1839	12	11	1	5
1840	12	10	2	3
1841	10	9	1	5
1842	5	4	1	3
	64	51	13	24

The Cups were won as follows: at Newcastle 6; at Doncaster 4; at Catterick 3; at Richmond 3; at Stockton 2; at Northallerton 2, and one each at Ascot, Chester, Lancaster and Lincoln.

With the standard of racing so high, Newcastle became very popular. The *Sporting Magazine* of 1838 reported 'Newcastle is decidedly the most increasing and prosperous meeting in Her Majesty's Dominions. It has become so by the spirited efforts of their excellent clerk of the course, Mr James Radford'. The Town Moor had come a long way from the 'milk and water affair' of the past. Writing in 1852 in *The Sportsman*, Druid commented 'Newcastle still holds its own but it has this sad peculiarity, that however good the entries be, nearly everything is scratched before the first bell rings!'

By 1866, the sharp practice still prevailed, and prompted this comment in *Baily's Magazine* 'The Meeting at Newcastle certainly eclipses all others for the unblushing and disreputable robberies perpetrated upon the public by owners of animals engaged in the Northumberland Plate. Although nearly a score of horses had been in the betting, the event proved that not more than three or four were ever really meant ... how the owners can possibly reconcile such nefarious doings and atrocious turpitude with common decency, we are at a loss to conceive'. Duplicity often backfired on the crafty owners. Inheritress won the Plate in 1845 but in doing so had 'again disappointed her party by winning when they did NOT expect her to, whereas at Ascot she lost when she should have won'.

The first song that Geordie Ridley of *Blaydon Races* fame ever wrote was about a horse in the Northumberland Plate called Joey Jones who triumphed in 1861 shortly after the great Underhand had notched a hat-trick of victories. The horse was owned locally by a Mr Stewart, and proved a popular winner at 10–1.

Ridley's chorus went:

Oh, he jogs along,
he cantered along,
he licked them all sae fine.
He was bred at Gateshead,
he's the pride O'Coaly Tyne.

Eventually it was the double-dealing owners and the emergence of a criminal element among racegoers that prompted the move from the Town Moor to Gosforth Park. Charles Perkins and Fife Scott bought High Gosforth House from the Brandlings, a highly respected North-East sporting family, and formed the Gosforth Park Company in 1881.

Town Moor Winners 1849 – 1881

Date	Owner	Winner	Date	Owner	Winner
1849	Mr Eddison's	John Crosser	1866	J Johnstone's	Rococo
1850	Lord Eglington's	Elthiron	1867	Mr Montgomery's	Fervacques
1851	T Wilkinson's	Neasham	1868	Captain Gray's	Fortunio
1852	Mr Melklam's	Stilton	1869	Mr Bowes's	The Spy
1853	Mr Morris's	Kingston	1870	Mr York's	Kennington
1854	Mr Milner's	Grapeshot	1871	Mr Bowes's	Taraban
1855	Mr Mather's	Whitelock	1872	Mr Henderson's	Spenithorne
1856	Lord Zetland's	Zeta	1873	Mr Holdsworth's	Falkland
1857	G Forster's	Underhand	1874	J Snarry's	Lily Agnes
1858	G Forster's	Underhand	1875	Mr Holme's	Harriet Laws
1859	G Forster's	Underhand	1876	Lord Rosebery's	Snail
1860	Mr Whittaker's	First Lord	1877	F G Hobson's	Hampton
1861	Mr Stewart's	Joey Jones	1878	R C Vyner's	Glastonbury
1862	Mr Marshall's	Montebello	1879	Mr R Cowan's	Clearhead
1863	W I'Anson's	Caller Ou	1880	R C Vyner's	Micenae
1864	W I'Anson's	Caller Ou	1881	Mr Jardine's	Bonnie Doon
1865	Mr McKenzie's	Brown Bread	*(Last race on Town Moor)*		

BENSON'S OFFICIAL CARD

OF

NEWCASTLE-UPON-TYNE
SUMMER MEETING 1881.

STEWARDS : The Right Hon. the Earl of Durham: Charles Perkins, Esq.; The Right Hon. the Earl of Rosebery; The Most Noble the Marquis Talon; R.C.Vyner, Esq.; The Right Hon. the Earl of Zetland.

Mr. Thomas Craggs of Stockton-on-Tees, *Secretary, Clerk of the Course and Stakeholder.*
Mr. W. J. Ford, of Nottingham, *Judge, Clerk of the Scales, and Handicapper.*
Mr. James Hedley, *Starter.*

NEWMARKET RULES STRICTLY IN FORCE AT THIS MEETING.

WEDNESDAY, JUNE 29, 1881.

4·0 The NORTHUMBERLAND PLATE of 500 sov., in money, added to a Handicap Sweepstakes of 25 sovs. each.

Weights published June 1st. at 10a.m.   Forfeits declared at Noon on the 7th. June.
Weights raised 2 lb.

1	Mr. R. Jardine's ch c Teviotdale, 4yrs .... (in. 12 lb ex) 9 0	*Dark blue, silver braid.*
2	Mr. J. Pickersgill's b h Robbie Burns, 5yrs 8 12	*Green, white seams.*
3a	Mr Vyner's b h Mycenæ, 5yrs 8 3	*Mauve cerise.*
4a	Lord Durham's b h Ridotto, 6yrs 8 2	*Purple straw sleeves & cap.*
5a	Lord Rosebery's ch c Prudhomme, 4yrs 8 2	*Primrose and rose hoops.*
6	Mr. Norman's ch c Incendiary, 4yrs 7 13	*Chocolate, red cap.*
7a	Mr. W. Stephenson's b f Novice, 4yrs 7 9	*Yellow, black belt and cap.*
8a	Mr. R. Jardine's b c Bonnie Doon, 4yrs 7 3	*Dark blue, silver braid.*
9	Mr. R. Jardine's b h Blackthorn, 5yrs 7 0	*Dark blue, silver braid.*
10	Mr. R. Peek's b c Sirdar, 4yrs 6 13	*Blue, orange sleeves.*
11a	Mr. J. Smith's b g Mars, aged 6 12	*Blue, white stars.*
12a	Mr. J. Pickersgill's b c Dominic, 4yrs 6 9	*Green, white seams.*
13a	Mr. R.C.Vyner's ch c Hagioscope, 3yrs 6 0	*Violet, white belt.*
14a	Marquis Talon's ch h Triumvir, 5yrs 5 12	*Blue, black cap.*
15	Mr. J. Martin's b c Loonie, 3yrs 5 11	

Early Days at Gosforth Park

At the time that horseracing in Newcastle was being transferred from the Town Moor to Gosforth in 1881, a *Newcastle Journal* reporter forecast that the Park's distance from town would put an end to the traditional Race Sunday Parade 'to all practical intents and purposes the Turf History of Newcastle enters upon a new epoch tomorrow when the first summer meeting as promoted by the High Gosforth Park Company will be placed on trial'.

The Northumberland Plate of 1882 was the first of 59 Plates to be run at Gosforth on the Wednesday of Race Week. It was by no means favoured by the public. For 49 years Geordie had got in for nowt, less betting losses, on the Town Moor. Up till then he'd left questions of finance to the gentry. But the new management could never hope to pay their way on that basis.

The Brandling estate had been bought for £60,000 and the 805 acres which constituted the Park transferred to 'a body of speculators actuated with a desire to promote sport in a proper fashion and get a fair return for their trouble and outlay'.

Outraged letters were despatched to local newspapers insisting that 'Gosforth should remain sacred to all the wild fowl and exclusiveness of a country gentleman's residence'. Flat and chase courses were laid down, stands erected and stabling for 100 horses; for the Press 'a new room for the fourth estate and a private enclosure in the stands'. The Newcastle Borough Engineer expressing concern over the erection of the stands, tested them with a gang of men and pronounced them capable of carrying 10 to 20 times the number they were intended to accommodate.

All was ready for the Spring Meeting of 1882 taking place on April 10th and 11th: charge 6d. 'A reasonable charge which despite its distance from town should not deter masses from being present'. The day went very well and the only quibble was that 'the course lacked herbage and clay was showing in places'. This minor hiccup was rectified for the very first running of the Northumberland Plate at Gosforth when 'the course was coated with a soft yielding covering, which will be found extremely grateful to horses in the event of the weather being dry'. It bucketed down! 'Within the past fortnight we have had a sufficiency of rain, thunder and lightning to serve us for a month at least'. In spite of the rain 50,000 people came racing that week, with charges being as follows:

	Week	Tues	Wed	Thurs
Park	–	6d	1/-	6d
Grandstand	21/-	7/6	10/-	7/6
Paddock	10/6	5/-	5/-	5/-

Transport to the Park was the major problem and the railways carried 7,000 passengers between Newcastle Central Station and Killingworth on 34 special trains. The more affluent paid a sovereign for a cab. That first Race Week was patronised by gentry who stayed at the Park Hotel where Mr Phillips, the manager,

16

had 'wine cellars fitted with Pommery, Heidsicker, Moet and Chandon, while his culinary stores were big enough to feed an ordinary-sized town for a week'.

The first Plate winner was not received with enthusiasm. At the first acceptance Faugh-A-Ballagh was installed as a hot favourite and started at 5–4. It led for most of the way but fell back to be unplaced to Mr H Bragg's Victor Emanuel carrying 8st who was returned at 100–9. A 12 length second was W Stevenson's Novice, with R C Cook's Champion another half a length away, third. It was noted that the rest of the field were pulled up a long way from home!

The great Fred Archer came up to Newcastle to ride the following year's winner Barcaldine under the steadier of 9st 10lb. The horse, unbeaten in every race it contested, won in spite of having to spend three hours before the race with its suspect leg in a bucket of cold water. Barcaldine had been the subject of a major scandal two years earlier when entered for the Plate on the Town Moor. Its owner then, an Irishman called George Low, had been warned off for trying to persuade Sir John Astley to part with £1,000 in exchange for a promise not to run Barcaldine. Low was banned *sine die* and the horse withdrawn.

First Plate Winners at High Gosforth Park

	strs	owner	winner	jockey
1882	11	Mr H Bragg	Victor Emanuel	Platt
1883	10	Mr R Peck	Barcaldine	Fred Archer
1884	9	Mr T Holmes	Lawminster	J Fagan
1885	7	Mr R Craig	Blue Grass	Giles
1886	6	R C Vyner	Stoneclink	Goodway
1887	13	Mr W Blake	Exmoor	J Watts
1888	10	Mr C Perkins	Matin Bell	Chandley
1889	7	Lord Durham	Drizzle	Blake
1890	12	Mr J Lowther	Houndsditch	Morgan
1891	11	Major Joicey	Queen's Birthday	J Watts
1892	8	Mr I'Anson	Newcourt	Mullen
1893	5	Lord Hastings	Seaton Delaval	F Finlay
1894	8	Mr Buchanan	Newcourt	Colling
1895	9	Mr Buchanan	The Docker	F Finlay
1896	5	Mr C Perkins	Dare Devil	J Fagan
1897	15	Mr Calvert	Bradwardine	C Wood
1898	10	R C Vyner	King Crow	F Black
1899	7	Lord Durham	Sherburn	F Rickaby

'To See the Blaydon Races'

The origin of the Blaydon Races is obscure. It is almost certain that races were held there from the middle of the eighteenth century, probably more as a flapping track than anything else. They were revived in 1861, being held on Whit Mondays and occasional August Bank Holiday Mondays.

The *Racing Calendar* of 1861 shows that the races were governed not by Jockey Club rules but those laid down by British Racing Club regulations. They had the backing of fine reputable sportsmen, but as meetings degenerated into rowdy affairs pandering to beer tents, gambling stalls and side shows, gradually the men of repute withdrew their patronage.

The Races were held on a circular course at Stella Haughs destined to become Stella South Power Station. The 1862 meeting referred to in Geordie Ridley's song, was 'Over Blaydon Island, Four Miles from Newcastle and within a Quarter Mile of the Railway Station'. It was recorded 'the course which is nearly a mile in circumference, is situated in a breezy and cool position locked in the embrace of Father Tyne'.

The rules of racing were brief 'Three horses to start for each of the races or the added money will not be given. No person to ride except in proper jockey costume. All disputes will be settled by the Stewards. Fees payable to the clerk of the course: 5/- each entry.'

A fine painting commemorating the 1862 Blaydon Races now hangs in the Gosforth Park Hotel Close scrutiny will reward the viewer with sight of all the main people mentioned in the song. One of the rare personalities of the day was Coffee Johnny, always at the races and always '*with his white hat on*'.

According to his grandson Joe Oliver of Swalwell, Johnny, an habitual coffee drinker, was a blacksmith at Winlaton. He was a great follower of the hounds and the races and, being something of a dandy, he used to wear an enormous top hat. A fine handsome man in his pure white headgear, Johnny was the man to spot a mile away.

It was said that Coffee Johnny saved the life of the young daughter of Lord Ravensworth who, whenever they met after that, would give him a gold sovereign as a token of his bravery. He made the good lord laugh one day when he bragged 'The day will come my lord, when I will own more land than you.' 'How is that?' queried his lordship. 'Well,' said the six feet six Johnny, 'I'm a big man and it'll take more land to bury me than thee.'

Born in 1800, Coffee Johnny lived for another 40 years after the song which immortalised him. He died in the town of Blyth and when his body was being relayed back to Winlaton, the village band played '*When Johnny Comes Marching Home*'.

The Blaydon Races continued intermittently until 1916, when a two-day meeting was sanctioned by the Ministry of Munitions who granted the workers on Tyneside a holiday.

Upwards of 4,000 people turned up for the first day's racing on September 1st, when the Company was able to advance 'a goodly sum' to the British Sportsmen's Ambulance Fund. On the second day, however, it was the crowd who needed the ambulances when in torrential rain, a state of public disorder was in evidence. Rioting occurred when a horse named Anxious Moments was involved in a disputed decision, resulting in furious backers tearing up their tickets, the weighing room and everything which moved, before despatching the lot into the River Tyne.

It was to be the last of the Blaydon Races.

The Northumberland Plate is now presented to the winning owner each year.

Made by Northern Goldsmith's of Newcastle, the trophy's centre-piece depicts the Percy Lion of Northumberland.

Bee'swing, pride of Northumberland.

A very ornate Town Moor grandstand in 1867.

Seaton Delaval goes to post in the 1893 Northumberland Plate.

Crowds at the annual Race Sunday Parade.

"Coffee Johnny had his white hat on," but at Gosforth in 1900 it was flat caps and bowlers.

Flappers at Gosforth in the 20s.

Alec Taylor trained Elizabetta in 1910 (left). Jack Watts saddled Show Girl in 1930 (right).

Workers at Gosforth Park earned five shillings in the 1920s.

Son-in-Law (above) was bred by Reg Day (left), then produced Foxlaw to win in 1926. From the same blood-line came Sweet Story, 40 years later .

(Above) Oracion wins for Tommy Weston in 1939.

(Below) Not a fence in sight as Gusty wins the 1946 Northumberland Plate at Aintree.

Pitmen used to stage their own Derby 1,000 feet below ground.

Doug Smith (left) and brother Eph, won five Plates between them.

27

First time around in 1948. R Robson's Impressive with Tony Holloway up.

Two short-heads and a neck, in a driving 1948 finish.

George Boyd (left) also trained New Brig and Cagirama, while Willie Snaith rode Fol Ami to win in 1949.

Massive crowds flocked to Gosforth just after the war (above).

Willie Nevett (left) was Cock o' the North then. Charlie Elsey was champion trainer in 1956.

The 1952 winner was a handicap certainty.

Sir Gordon Richards wins on Friseur in 1953.

Top jockeys of the 1950s Weighing Out.

Hide and Starkey were the young pretenders then.

*Murless (above left) had a hat-trick of Plate winners. Bill Dutton (above right) rode a
Grand National winner before he trained Great Rock in 1957.
Jack Colling (below left) and Joe Mercer were responsible for Master of Arts, 1958.*

Charlie Elsey entertains his patrons, including (seated) Phil Bull and Lord Allendale.

Randolph Gibson surveys the damage to the Grandstand in 1962.

Trained Peacock, Ridden W Nevett

Willie Nevett was the Pitmen's Champion long before Arthur Scargill had seen his first shaft bottom! Born in Chorley, Lancashire, in 1906, Nevett was apprenticed at 14 when he went to Middleham Manor House to ride for three generations of Peacocks who made their mark in northern racing. The first Peacock to train a Plate winner at Newcastle was Dobson Peacock who saddled ale-drinking Palmy Days in 1904 two years before Nevett was born. Five years later in 1909 he trained Sir Harry to win for Mr D Jardine in a field of 11.

M Dobson Peacock born in 1856, was an amateur jockey at the time he took over at Spigot Lodge, Middleham, from Henry Hall. Nevett's father had been a stable lad with Hall so it seemed only natural that young Willie, one of 11 children, should serve his apprenticeship there.

One winner that Dobson himself rode over the sticks at Catterick in 1877 was John Osborne's Charlie Boy. He recalled that the jockeys had to get changed in a tent that day. Osborne, a member of a Suffolk family who had migrated to Yorkshire, was no mean horseman himself and rode in 37 consecutive Epsom Derbys, winning in 1868 on Pretender. He became known as 'Old Pusher' riding very short, and when asked why he rode shorter than the legendary Fred Archer, he gave the obvious answer 'Because my legs aren't as long as his'. John Osborne continued riding well into his eighties, as he supervised the training of his horses on the Yorkshire Moors. Indeed he gave Mynora a pipe-opener before she won the 1912 Northumberland Plate.

Dobson Peacock whose staunchly patriotic advice was 'put your faith in Yorkshire horses, cricketers, pudding and beef', had to wait till 1923 for his next success in the Pitmen's Derby with Carpathus, ridden by Jack Ledson. It wasn't until the following year that Willie Nevett rode his first winner, Stockwood, at Carlisle, not for his guv'nor but Jim Adams, a supremely fit nonagenarian.

Yet another of the famous northern trainers, Neville Crump, tells of Dobson's remarkable judgement of form, when as a young schoolboy, Crump was given four horses to back at Edinburgh. 'These aren't tips you know, lad,' said crafty Dobson 'they WILL win'. And they did!

The life of an apprentice is never an easy one but Willie Nevett had it harder then most, being paid only £3 a year for a seven day week which commenced at half past five in the morning. There were certain perks: he got his first present from an appreciative owner when Sir Thomas Putnam gave him an autographed bible. It must have been generally acknowledged that apprentice jockeys were just one step away from damnation as the 14-times champion jockey George Fordman who weighed in at only 3st 12lbs in his youth, was presented with an identical bible and a whip engraved 'Honesty is the best policy'.

It seems not all jockeys at the turn of the century paid heed to the old adage but frittered away the small remuneration they did receive during their racing days, and were often left destitute when overtaken by weight and the devil Booze. Willie Nevett had no such problems! He was quiet, a non-drinker and was cautious with his money. He owed much for his solid abstemious nature to a Northumbrian lass Evelyn Smith of Bellingham, whose parents had taken a hotel in Middleham. Willie and his Evelyn were married and raised a family of two boys and a girl.

Nevett completed his 10-year apprenticeship in 1930 two years after he had won his first Northumberland Plate on Mr J G Thompson's Primrose League at the rewarding odds of 100–7. There were 14 runners that day which equalled the biggest turn-out for 30 years. No wonder Dobson Peacock had a smile on his face: he had already won the big race the year before with Border Minstrel to become the first trainer this century to turn out winners in consecutive years. Dobson died in 1935, leaving his son Matt to take over the reins at Manor Lodge.

Lancastrian Nevett began to get offers to move him and his talent for riding winners down south. Thankfully for northern racegoers he resisted the temptation, showing great loyalty to Middleham. For a couple of seasons he did accept a retainer from Lord Rosebery and rode a considerable amount of winners south of Watford.

Ten years after his first success in the Plate, he waved the flag for Charlie Elsey when he drove Union Jack home in 1938. And by an amazing coincidence, this victory occurred 50 years to the day after Nevett senior had led out the 1888 Plate winner Matin Bell, owned by Charlie Perkins, one of the men instrumental in moving Newcastle Races from the Town Moor to Gosforth Park seven years earlier.

It was back to the Peacock connection again for Willie when he won his third Derby in 1945, this time for Dobson's son Matt on the fabulous Dante. Nevett's two previous Derby successes were also gained during the war: 1941 on Owen Tudor and 1944 with Ocean Swell for Lord Rosebery. Both were chance rides. Fred Darling's stable jockey Gordon Richards was out of action in 1941 and Private W Nevett of the Royal Army Ordnance Corps stepped into the breech. In 1944 Eph Smith had the chance of riding the favourite Growing Confidence, and Lord Rosebery had given his permission to accept the mount. Plans went wrong and Smith again chose the wrong'un when he opted for the much-fancied Tehran. That year Nevett showed the world just how good a horseman he was by riding a great finish to get Ocean Swell home at Newmarket by a neck and a short head from Tehran and Happy Dancer.

Although never winning the unofficial Jockey's Championship, Nevett was always the best man to bet on in trebles and accumulators especially on the Scottish circuit. He rode in all six races at Edinburgh in 1934, won five of them and was placed in the other! On consecutive days at Ayr in 1947, he was in the winner's enclosure no fewer than four times each day. In 1954 Nevett notched up his 79th winner on the Ayr course since the war. And on July 11th of the same year on his favourite Gosforth Park course, he scored an amazing five out of five!

Matt Peacock, a man whose horses were always to be feared, died in July 1951, and *The Times* obituary recorded: 'It is as though a great tree has fallen and the landscape of race meetings will never be the same again'.

Matt's son, Dick Peacock, carried on with the family racing tradition but found some of the horses left by his father difficult to train. One such animal was Border Legend then owned by the Duke of Northumberland and earmarked for the 1952 Plate. Sadly for the Duke, the horse went wrong and was never entered, leaving him still without a success in the race which bears his name.

Richard Dobson Peacock died just four years ago, and mourners from all around the area gathered outside the fourteenth century church of St Mary and Alkalda. There was a traditional period of ten minutes set aside for the villagers to stand outside the Manor House and bid farewell to the last of that particular Peacock line.

Yet another Peacock, Matt's brother Harry, also became a household name at Gosforth Park, and the Richmond trainer's contribution to racing is commemorated by a prestigious Newcastle race which bears his name.

Willie Nevett was over 50 when he hung up his proverbial footwear which had booted home more than 2,000 winners. Home for the unassuming northern lad was destined to be Patrick Brompton, a large estate between Bedale and Middleham, where Willie was left in peace to become a bloodstock breeder and an expert grower of champion gladioli. But then ... once a champion ...

Early Twentieth Century Plate Winners

	strs	*trainer*	*winner*	*jockey*	*SP*
1900	8	Mr Dyer	Joe Chamberlain	J Martin	–
1901	12	G Lambton	Reminiscence	H Aylin	7–2
1902	10	P Peck	Osbech	W Halsey	9–2
1903	8	W I'Anson	Cliftonhall	B Dillon	2–1
1904	10	M Peacock	Palmy Days	T Heppell	3–1
1905	9	G Lambton	Princess Florizel	W Saxby	9–4
1906	12	R Colling	Outbreak	S Walkington	evens
1907	11	W Mathews	Killigrew	C Ringstead	100–8
1908	11	J Fagan	Old China	G McCall	10–1
1909	11	M Peacock	Sir Harry	O Madden	5–2
1910	11	A Taylor	Elizabetta	S Wooton	9–2
1911	10	W Robinson	Pilo	W Saxby	8–1
1912	9	J Osborne	Mynora	J Ledson	20–1
1913	13	G Lambton	The Tylt	F Rickaby	9–1
1914	9	J Osborne	The Guller	J Ledson	9–2
1915 – 1918		*No races*			
1919	6	G Lambton	Trestle	G Colling	6–1
1920	10	R W Colling	Irish Lake	P Jones	7–2
1921	12	P W Bewicke	Hunt Law	H Jones	5–1
1922	14	J Cannon	Double Hackle	H Robbins	5–1
1923	11	M D Peacock	Carpathus	J Ledson	4–1
1924	9	A Scott	Jazzband	C Smirke	5–1
1925	10	R W Colling	Obliterate	J Childs	3–1
1926	6	R Day	Foxlaw	M Beary	5–1
1927	7	M D Peacock	Border Minstrel	T Weston	3–1
1928	14	M D Peacock	Primrose League	W Nevett	100–7
1929	13	A Sadler	Ballynahinch	J Caldwell	10–1

Into The Back-Straight

As the North-East racing scene dipped its toes into the twentieth century it was noticeable that although it remained very popular, Northumberland's premier race was not attracting the high calibre animal which it had done in its infancy.

One exception was Lord Derby's Princess Florizel easy winner of the 1905 Plate carrying only 6st 7lb, and breaking the world record time for two miles by completing the course in 3 mins 25 ^{1}/s. The timing of horseraces at the turn of the century had not been reduced to anywhere near what might be called mathematic accuracy, and timing in England was recorded by a watch-holder in the stands. This caused the *Sporting Chronicle* to note in 1912 'that there is any actual value in the time-test is a moot point, and it is hard to believe some of the records'.

Towards the end of the nineteenth century there began a steady influx of overseas jockeys into England. Tod Sloan brought the short leather and low wind-resisting crouch style from America in 1897. His streamlined performances revolutionised the art of jockeyship in England, sparking off many imitators.

Roger Mortimer in his definitive book *'The Flat'* tells of how the little American always bragged that there was nothing he could not ride but shied away from a horse at Epsom when someone told him that the animal had a fiery temper and was difficult at the starting gate. Fred Rickaby, jockey of the 1899 Plate winner Sherburn and grandfather of Billy Rickaby, heard of this and told the trainer he would take the mount. He rubbed salt into Sloan's wounds by winning easily.

Some excellent riders from Australia began to dominate the English Turf. Probably the best of all was Frank Wooton who headed the jockeys' table for four consecutive years between 1909 – 1912. But it was his brother Stanley who was to make his mark at Newcastle by winning the 1910 Plate on Elizabetta after the pair had already captured the Chester Cup under the flyweight of 6st 11lb.

Elizabetta was trained by Alec Taylor who was as canny with his money as he was with his horses. A bachelor, he left £595,790 when he died in 1943. As a trainer he was a very patient man, but luckily his owners could afford to wait. He was of the opinion that horses were babies until they were three. It was this attitude which nursed Lemberg and Elizabetta to win the Epsom and Pitmen's Derby respectively in 1910.

In 1914 the last winner of the Plate before hostilities curtailed racing for four years, was John Osborne's The Guller ridden by J Ledson. The same combination had carried off the Chester Cup the previous year.

It was during this war that a great fire destroyed the Mansion House at Gosforth together with a large part of the grandstand. Almost £10,000 worth of damage was caused, but with the Northumberland Yeomanry being based inside the grounds, work on rebuilding had to take its turn. The military had free range of the buildings and surrounds for a flat-rate rent of £200 per month, plus damages!

The war over, the Northumberland Plate also had its share of tragedy when in 1919 in a field of six, Wildwood became tailed off as the horses entered the straight. As Lord Derby's subsequent winner Trestle stormed past the two furlong marker leading the field, a poor unwitting spectator, thinking all the horses had gone through, stuck his head out through the rails and was killed outright when Wildwood charged into him.

The year 1923 is memorable for only 50 paying spectators being in the Silver Ring for one day's racing as bookies staged a 'walk-out' in protest at a 10/- admission charge; and a new Tramway Route linking directly into Gosforth Park from Newcastle in 1924 coincided with Jazzband winning when ridden by Charlie Smirke. Jazzband was trained on a farm at Alnham in north Northumberland by its owner Adam Scott, and was the first Plate winner seen by Mrs Sylvia Taylor, first wife of the late Col Dick Taylor DSO, one-time Chairman of Directors at High Gosforth Park. She recalls: 'I was only young at the time, but remember that there was great excitement in the village at the time because of the horse winning. It won very easily. I was at the course, but I was far too young to understand what was going on. Charlie Sample's grandfather took me, but if I had my way they wouldn't allow children under five into the place: they just get under your feet! At one time the only way to get directly into the Park was by tram but now they all arrive in their Mercedes!'

Reg Day was a remarkable judge of stayers. He was responsible for running and breeding Son-in-Law who sired Foxlaw to win the Plate in 1926. Foxlaw carried on the great tradition, winning the Ascot Gold Cup the following year and later siring Foxhunter and Tiberius who also won Ascot's premier prize in 1933 and 1935 respectively.

One of the oldest of the bookies still to frequent the Park is 72 year old W C Stewart of Gateshead. 'I was a bookie's clerk for my father in 1928 when Primrose League won for Willie Nevett. My father had been a newspaper seller on the Shields Road before he became a bookie. He had served in the Coldstream Guards in the first war and I did the same in the second! There was a lot more people went racing in those days but then the wagers were obviously not as high. My first day's clerking was when I was 15 and we must have taken about £250 on the Plate that day which we thought was very good, whereas they talk in thousands now. The winner was 100–7 so it was a good day for us and I think I got about 25 bob. You could hardly get me to speak to anyone after that: I thought I was so well off!'

The year 1929 saw the famous cricketer 'Ranji' lead in Ballynahinch who had been runner-up to Border Minstrel two years earlier.

Jack Watts who trained Show Girl to win the 1930 Plate was a member of a famous racing family. His father, also called Jack, rode four Epsom Derby winners and had one Pitmen's Derby victory with Queen's Birthday, in 1887. Jack Jnr continued where Jack Snr left off, riding numberous winners over a period of years including a five-timer at Windsor. In 1936 he left England to train for Frenchman Marcel Boussac, but come back in 1940 after France fell to the

Germans and later took over the training of Jim Joel's horses at Foxhill.

Show Girl's jockey Charlie Elliott was right at his peak in the 1920s and 30s, sharing top-jock with Steve Donoghue in 1923, and going on to win three Derbys on Call Boy, Bois Roussel and Nimbus. Almost at the end of his career he was connected with Souepi's victories in the Gold Cup and the Goodwood Cup, but it was H Packham who had the mount when Souepi took the Northumberland Plate in 1952.

Another fine rider was locally-born Willie Bullock. It was he who partnered Capt Charles Elsey's Leonard in 1933, having previously won the Epsom Derby on the complete outsider Signoretta at 100–1 in 1908. Bullock's brother Tom was an excellent trainer of greyhounds, and was invited to set up a course within the Park with the object of establishing the sport. Two fields were let to the Bullock family and they occupied a house at Gosforth East Lodge for a great many years. Rabbits were brought in from Killingworth to stock the fields one of which is still known as the Coursing Field. Ralph Bullock, Willie's nephew, now lives in Seahouses, and he recalls: 'Willie came up from Malton to stay with us at the Gosforth Lodge during Race Week. For that particular race he had to shed a few pounds on the day because Leonard was only set to carry 7st 9lbs and that was way under Willie's riding weight. My father Tom paced him around the track with Willie sweating off his excess weight under two overcoats and two pairs of trousers. It must have worked because the horse won easily at 100–7.'

Northumbrian John A Marshall, former trainer and steward at Gosforth and now a Director, says that most of the Plate winners of the 30s were taken up by the Northumberland Lighthorse Breeders Society for stud purposes: 'I got my interest from my father who bred horses,' John says, 'and Leonard and Ballynahinch, are two names that spring to mind, as well as the Duke of Northumberland's Carnival Boy, although he didn't win the Plate. I trained up at Chatton in the 1940s and 50s – mostly over the sticks – and I suppose my biggest success was on the stud side when I bred Bally Atom, the winner of what is now known as the Arkle Chase at Cheltenham'.

Plate Winners in the 1930s

	strs	trainer	winner	jockey	SP
1930	12	J Watts	Show Girl	C Elliott	100–8
1931	8	I Anthony	Blue Vision	K Gethin	11–4
1932	10	M D Peacock	Pomarrel	J Dines	8–1
1933	10	C F Elsey	Leonard	W Bullock	100–7
1934	15	J Jarvis	Whiteplains	E Smith	25–1
1935	8	H Cottrill	Doreen Jane	D Smith	15–8
1936	7	R C Dawson	Coup de Roi	E Smith	5–2
1937	11	F Armstrong	Nectar II	P Maher	100–8
1938	12	C F Elsey	Union Jack	W Nevett	10–1
1939	13	G Lambton	Oracion	T Weston	9–1

If not in racing excellence then in matters of ladies' high fashion, Newcastle Races began to vie with Ascot just before the Second World War. It was reported 'Rhododendron blooms, jockeys and ladies' gowns were merged into the neutral tint of the sky ... the Sheriff of Newcastle was present with Mrs Grantham, whose reindeer rep suit was worn with a skunk stole and a fawn hat; Mrs Arthur Lowe the Deputy Lady Mayoress, wore rosewood rep with her sables; Mrs May Easten last year's Lady Mayoress was neatly costumed in fawn'.

In 1937, Princess Florizel's two mile record was broken asunder by the Sam Armstrong-trained Nectar II. Jockey Paddy Maher put his foot down to such extent that the unbelievable time of 3 mins 22.00 secs still stands as a record to this day. Armstrong, a great trainer of outstanding stayers, also saddled two more Plate winners: Fol Ami in 1949 with Willie Snaith up and Sycomore II ridden by Edgar Britt in 1951.

The last Plate winner before another war broke out was George Lambton's Oracion. This was the only time that stylish jockey Tommy Weston rode to victory in the race but for trainer Lambton it was all too familiar. Since he had turned out Reminiscence to win in 1901, the Honorable George had gained another *four* tremendous successes in Tyneside's premier race.

As Oracion swept past the post, many of those present at Gosforth Park must have wondered whethere there would be a Northumberland Plate in 1940. And happy racegoers bound for Byker, Blyth and Bedlington, on buying an *Evening Chronicle*, cast anxious eyes at the reports of world events that were to lead into yet another crazy war. For winning jockey Tommy Weston, it was to be his last big race win before he joined the Royal Navy.

High Gosforth Park was taken over by various armed service units during the war and many of the course facilities fell into an acute state of disrepair. They were not alone! A number of courses were commandeered: Scots Guards went into Kempton Park, and Coldstream Guards into Sandown. Because of the fear of air raids, the Doncaster St Leger was abandoned and no racing of any description took place until mid-October 1939.

Racing began again on a regional basis in 1942 but the only courses permitted to race were based at Newmarket, Salisbury, Windsor, Pontefract and Stockton. Northern horses were allowed only at Pontefract and Stockton.

A Jockey Club committee was set up in 1941 to inquire into the future of racing and its report recognised the shabby treatment which was being meted out to the two-bob each way punter: 'There is little doubt that in attractiveness from the point of view of the general public, racing today in England has fallen further behind that in other countries. And racecourse executives have shown very little disposition to cater for the individual outside the fringe of those directly concerned with the business of racing. Yet from this reservoir must be drawn the increased attendances which we seek, for from it must come a large part of the new money required to bring about the improvements which are called for.'

However well-intentioned the Jockey Club, it was soon obvious that under a tentative post-war Labour government the policy would be 'softly-softly'. This was a pity for there was very little else for the man in the street to spend his money on: holidays abroad were not permitted; cars were unobtainable and anyway there was no petrol; alcohol was very scarce and clothes and household furniture were rationed. The *Bloodstock Breeders' Review* stated: 'There has never been such crowds, such enthusiasm, such big fields, such prosperity, in the sales rings as well as that in the stands and enclosures.' It was a boom time for racing and gambling, but the extra revenue failed to find its way into the right projects and a great chance was lost.

After the Allies' victory in 1945 a degree of normality fell upon the picturesque High Gosforth Estate, and work commenced on dismantling the ugly Nissen Huts and getting the Park into its racing colours once more. Clerk of the course Randolph Gibson proved himself the man for the job.

Bulldozers and excavators moved in supported by a fleet of lorries. Great care was taken to preserve the topsoil, and the whole of the ground was thoroughly cultivated. Apart from the work out on the course, a hugh restoration programme took place on the stands. Just about every building had been used by the Army, with all the attendant disastrous consequences that kind of occupation implies.

Renovation was slow, and the first running of the Northumberland Plate after the war in 1946 had to be transferred to Liverpool. The Scousers were uninterested in the big Geordie race, and only five horses turned out with Gusty the 7–4 favourite and Tregor at 9–4 being the only two to attract any money. Tregor cut out the early pace, but it was obvious from a long way out that Harry Wagg was living up to his nickname of Head Waiter and Gusty went on to win by a comfortable length.

It was ironic that a Northumbrian owner and Gosforth Park steward, Lord Allendale, should have to go to Aintree to see the horse, which was trained by C F Elsey, win the first post-war Northumberland Plate.

Charles Elsey had to wait until he was 75 before he became the first trainer from the north to head the trainers' list this century in 1956, a success which could not have been more popular amongst all sections of the racing community, for there were few men better liked.

Elsey's first job had been with his father who had in excess of 100 horses at Baumber, Lincs. In 1911 when he was thirty, Charles set up on his own at Middleham and ended up at Malton via Ayr. It was here that Capt Elsey – he had joined the Yorkshire Hussars in 1914 – began a distinguished Turf history and close assocation with Northumberland. As well as Lord Allendale, Elsey trained horses for Miss Jane Clayton who was from an old Northumbrian family. His first Plate win had been in 1933 with Leonard, and his second was with Union Jack, ridden by Willie Nevett in 1938.

Scottish trainer George Boyd who had a string of horses at Dunbar, won the 1948 Plate with Pappatea ridden by Harry Blackshaw who later became a successful trainer at Middleham. 'Harry always said Pappatea was the best horse he rode,' said Boyd. 'It meant so much to him.'

It was natural that George should become a horseman like his father John. Brought up in his father's stables at Peebles and later Westbarns, Dunbar, George assisted his brother Alec when John Boyd died in 1936. George went into the RAF and took over the Dunbar stables of 27 horses in 1947. His first winner was Backbite at Bogside in the April and three days later he followed that up with a treble at Edinburgh.

He went on to become Scotland's most successful trainer, winning two more Pitmen's Derbys in the 1960s with New Brig and Cagirama. 'New Brig was a good stayer and I suppose Cagirama was the least talented of my three Plate winners,' recalled Boyd. Harry Blackshaw proved how versatile he was later that year at Manchester when he rode in a flat race, hurdle and steeplechase in the course of one afternoon.

Cagirma had another couple of tilts after his Plate win of 1965 but without further success. Wendy Scott, who is now with the Druridge Bay Campaign, had the job of looking after Cagirama when he went to stud. 'He was a right mean character who would bite you as soon as look at you. It was a laugh at the St Boswell stud because 'Cagi' was so small he had to stand on a muck-heap to serve his mares,' she said.

Boyd's biggest and most controversial win was with Rockavon who won the 1961 Two Thousand Guineas at the enormous odds of 66–1. This was the first Scottish-trained horse to win the race, but Boyd missed seeing his finest training success because of a fog-bound Glasgow airport. Rockavon only won one more race: a match against a moderate animal at Newcastle.

Jack Fawcus was yet another rider/trainer with a fine Northumbrian tradition. As far back as 1832 in a race for amateur riders at Newcastle Town Moor, there is mention of Major St Paul's The Skipper, ridden by J Fawcus 'the best gentlemen rider in the north, Mr Fawcus made severe running all the way and was never headed in a most exciting race'.

Born at Dunstan Steads, Embleton, in 1908, Jack Fawcus was brought up on his father's farm and rode his first winner as an amateur in 1927. He served in the Northumberland Fusiliers in the Second World War, was taken prisoner and when repatriated in 1944 was a physical wreck. He found that his father had died and that the farm had been sold. Taking over the stables at Ashgill, Middleham, Capt Jack Fawcus's early patrons included J V Rank and Lord Joicey. His most notable successes were two victories in the Scottish Grand National. Jack Fawcus died in 1967 following a car crash on the way to Uttoxeter races. He was 59.

Post-War Plate Winners

Date	winner	owner	trainer	jockey	SP
1939 – 1945	*No races*				
1946	Gusty	Lord Allendale	C F Elsey	H Wragg	7–4
1947	Culrain	G Cullington	T Hall	D Smith	9–2
1948	Pappatea	R Simpson	G Boyd	H Blackshaw	20–1
1949	Fol Ami	M'ranee of Baroda	F Armstrong	W Snaith	9–2
1950	Light Cavalry	A MacLeod	M Everitt	J Sime	10–1
1951	Sycomore II	Maharaji of Morvi	F Armstrong	E Britt	9–4
1952	Souepi	G Digby	G Digby	H Packham	4–5
1953	Nick La Rocca	F Williams	J Colling	J Mercer	9–4
1954	Friseur	Mrs R Ryan	N Murless	G Richards	7–1
1955	Little Cloud	Sir V Sassoon	N Murless	L Piggott	15–2
1956	Jardiniere	T Lilley	N Murless	D Smith	2–1
1957	Great Rock	Mrs A Straker	W Dutton	E Hide	10–1
1958	Master of Arts	J Astor	J Colling	J Mercer	7–2
1959	Cannabiere	E Walker	A Barclay	D Morris	100–7

Trained R Robson at High Gosforth Park

The only professional trainer to use High Gosforth Park as a base was Ronnie Robson, now retired. Ronnie served in the Army during the last war but he was released on compassionate grounds when his brother, then training at Stocksfield, died suddenly from a cerebral haemorrage at only 26 years of age. Twenty-one year old Ronnie had been in the Army for four years before Lord Allendale at Bywell was instrumental in getting him a licence.

'At that time I was probably the youngest licence holder in training. Living in Stocksfield, it was through Lord Allendale, that the approach was made. In those days Allendale's horses were trained by Matt Peacock. His brother, Harry Peacock, trained at Hurgill Lodge at Richmond and Matt trained at Middleham. They both trained many winners.

'We won the Perkins Memorial Trophy twice with Prince Curnan. That particular trophy spent all the war years in the window of the Northern Goldsmiths on Newcastle main street. My brother had always admired that trophy during the war and when he died my father thought he had the animal that could win it. It was just as much for sentimental reasons as anything else that we tried to win it.

'Prince Curnan was owned by L G Maller of Gosforth; he was a retired ship's engineer. We won it two years running with the same horse. Northern Goldsmiths wanted us to take the money instead of the trophy but we kept it; it was worth about 50 quid then. If you won a thousand pound race in those days, you won a good race.

'It was while we were still at Stocksfield in 1948 that we had a go at winning the Plate with a horse called Impressive that I bought from Geordie Boyd. We only had about 7 st to carry and I arranged for a young apprentice from the Midlands, Tony Holloway, who had ridden a lot of winners for Bob Ward, to come up and ride for us. He stayed for a week before racing, getting to know the horse: he was just a young boy. Impressive was owned by a Newcastle bookmaker Tom Coates. The horse wasn't bought with the Plate in mind; he really was a mile to a mile and a quarter horse but then as time progressed we knew he'd get a bit further.

'Impressive was a big price. I shouldn't really have run him because he got cholic the night before, but I thought we'd let him take his chance. The only instructions I gave were that as long as the horse was going well within himself to try to make his weight tell because he would be getting two and a half stone from the eventual winner, Pappatea, and if you have that kind of weight advantage you've got to do something about it, there's no use in sitting alongside them.

'We hadn't set him out especially for the race but it was just one of those things that happened; he seemed to stay quite well and we thought he would get the two-mile. Most north-country people have a burning ambition to win the Plate and I was no different; it's almost classed as winning the Derby up here..

'There were some very good horses came to Newcastle to win the Plate, it's a pity that those days seem to have gone. But racing isn't the same; the Plate meetings then were occasions when everybody put on their best bib and tucker; the women all got dressed up, and that used to cost everybody a fortune for new outfits, but that was the name of the game. It became a big social occasion. But now, well ...

'Massive crowds came to the Plate meetings then and it was very very popular. For anyone who was interested in racing it was a wonderful week. In the early days all the horses came up by train. Specials came into the Killingworth Station and lots of south-country horses came up. It was quite a ritual in the morning getting up to watch horses work on the course. Lots and lots of people came up and they had huge crowds.

'In the old days all the southern trainers would get together and put their horses on a rail special at Newmarket. Then the special stopped at Killingworth Station and they walked them up to the course. It created great excitement. People like Jack Jarvis and Lord Rosebery came up regularly.

'Around 1950 I left Stocksfield and came to train at High Gosforth Park. I moved for the better facilities; I was persuaded by Randolph Gibson who was clerk of the course then, a wonderful fella! They had these derelict stables and he was keen to have somebody establish a training place inside the Park and help with runners etc.

'There had been stables there for the Renwick family; a private little yard for when they brought their horses. They were in a mess but we tarted them up and got them going. But having said that, the facilities in the Park were still inadequate for training horses. All right for having a bit of fun with a few. I only ever had up to a couple of dozen animals and even with that number I was struggling.

'In those days there were facilities for getting a bit of work on the back side of the course. But as time progressed there were more and more meetings; Mr Gibson retired and the facilities were no longer available. The opportunities for working on the course weren't there and we were only left with about 50 acres: barely adequate for doing the job. Doing it as a business was hardly on. But I stuck it for 25 years and we had a lot of success: not with horses of quality but quantity of winners we turned out.

'We bought new stock mainly at the Newmarket December Sales. I used to get an order to go from my owners and I went around the smaller studs. If you paid £1, 000 for a horse that was a lot of money! I paid £200 pounds for a horse called Charlie Proper and it won 18 races; old King Eider cost £1,000 and he won about 16 times; I bought Why tell who belonged to Winston Churchill, trained by Walter Nightingall, and gave £700 for him and he won 15 races. We used to go down to Newmarket to the biggest stables who were clearing out their back-end two year olds that hadn't come up to the qualities required. They had an influx of new horses coming in so they cleared out the rest. We all used to look for one that was bred to go over a trip that needed maybe another year and a bit longer race. But as the years wore on we found we were all looking for the same horse!

'In the late 50s Charlie Proper and King Eider were supposed to run in the Northumberland Plate. But it was just about the time when the new system for entering horses came in and I clean forgot to enter them at the last stage. Because I never had such a thing as secretarial staff! I had a very competent wife whom I relied on for the book work. In those days getting the entries in was a once-a-week job on a Sunday. That day appeared to be a marathon by the time you got through it. Seeing to all the horses in the morning then chatting to your owners who tended to visit you on a Sunday morning. And when you got over that you had to start doing your entries for the following week so that they would all get down to London for the Tuesday deadline. There were no rest days in racing: it was a seven-days-a-week job. But you had a choice: you either did it or you didn't.

'Willie Carson used to ride for us a lot. He was apprenticed in those days to Sam Armstrong. He was a wonderful man with his apprentices and there was never any problem if you wanted them to come up to Newcastle; he would send them up, fly the up, get them up by hook or by crook. We used to run horses as far down as Liverpool to about 150 miles into Scotland at Bogside. There were a lot of meetings to get through!

'I think training in a small way, you had to gamble; the profit margin wasn't there; I think I gambled all of my life! Although I never got it out of proportion but had to gamble in order to survive. The training fees were terribly small and travelling expenses for horseboxes were … today they talk in telephone numbers! Racing then was mainly for the sport, where you met a lot of nice people. A couple of friends could get together and buy a horse: up to four people were allowed in partnership. I don't know how I could cope nowadays with the syndicates they've got.

'I remember when starting stalls first came to Gosforth – about 1967 – I hated the sight of 'em! In the early days when they still used the starting gate, I had the use of the mile and a quarter gate on the course over on the far side. And it was great! But when the stalls came along you had to buy or make a set. We had this home-made arrangement with three boxes: a right Heath Robinson affair when you just pulled a lever and out they came … in theory. It was like bloody greyhound racing! I still prefer the old gate start!

'I think outside trainers liked Gosforth Park in the early days; I'm not all that sure if they like it now. Newcastle isn't getting the support that it should get; whether they need to think again about the conditions of some of the races, well … they are trying to attract the better-class horses but unfortunately it has not been successful.

'We have reached the stage today where Newcastle is struggling for survival! It should be a flower-bedecked place where people pay a minimum amount of money to go in; the facilities for horses and staff should be far in excess of what they are. It needs an awful lot of money but there is too much money being taken out of racing. I think they will *have* to redevelop the course otherwise the Park will go to the wall! It's very simple; it's not a profitable situation. The crowds are totally inadequate and it's sad. But it's too expensive! If a husband and wife want to go racing, by the time they get there, pay their entrance money and have a sandwich and a couple of bets … phew, they've spent the best part of 50 quid! And it's overpriced! I don't mean from the point of view of the Executive; it's because they haven't engendered sufficient revenue back into racing. MY biggest beef is with the bookmaking industry! I don't think they should ever have been allowed to have ALL the betting shops. There is plenty of room for bookies on the racecourse but the shops should have all been Tote-owned. If the government had allowed Tote offices in the first place then millions could have been ploughed back into the sport.

'I still think that many improvements could be made. When you go to a place like Newcastle, it's a Grade One course and it should be sparkling. Of course there are plenty of places worse. Go to the local jump meetings at Sedgefield or Hexham and the facilities are pre-historic! They're just barns dropping to bits! And you go in for something to eat and all they've got are mutton pies! Those days should be gone long since.

'You see, straight after the war people just accepted these conditions as being the norm. But then Randolph Gibson was instrumental in building the new stand and that was an excellent development. But that was the beginning and the end of it.

'Take now with all the money that is being ploughed in at Newmarket. Up here in the north we are *definitely* the poor relations! All the best horses are down south and I don't see that they are ever going to be able to put that right. Unfortunately they don't send all that many of their good horses up here.

'A lot of people give racing a bad name and they say this was done and that was done. In my lifetime racing was much cleaner than people try to make out. I'm not going to say wherever you get racing and gambling you will not get the odd few who will abuse it. You talk about non-triers, but even if they did knock skittles of daylights out of some of the horses they still couldn't have won.

'I don't regret any of it! It's a wonderful life with horses. I still go racing now and I wouldn't knock it in any shape or form!'

A Pitman's Derby

It's the end of another shift. The end of another week's graft, and you are riding outbye on the main belt stretched full-length on your belly travelling out from under the ploughed fields of Ashington Home Farm.

Near the shaft bottom, the free ride over, you hurl yourself from the rubber belt, scattering pieces of small coal on to the rocky ground of the narrow drift. Blinking away coal dust, the eyes focus on the thrupenny diddler of daylight at the top of the shaft, increasing in value as the cage nears the surface.

You stumble out into the sunshine, guarding eyes from the unaccustomed fierceness of the light, and fumble in an inside-jacket pocket for a watch encased for safety in a round metal tin. It's five minutes to twelve, and you glance around and see other miners of like mind hurrying towards the lamp cabin. Pulling the black pit-hat from your head, you tug the cap-lamp from its slot. Off comes the leather belt from which slides the heavy battery, left to clatter upon the shiny cobbles as you struggle to keep fustian trousers up with one free hand.

Join the queue at the lamp cabin, hobnailed boots shuffling impatiently all around. Your turn, and you place the lamp on a wooden bench and accept a small metal tally in return; your own private identity tag; proof that you are no longer down the pit; proof that you're safe … at least for another day.

The pit-head baths hadn't been built all that long. The mines were five years into nationalisation which had promised so much but achieved so little. No privacy in the communal showers, with a naked marra (mate) entering the cubicle to wash away the coal dust from your back. Some miners were superstitious and thought that washing the back too often was strength-sapping. They were the original unwashed!

Getting ready in the clean-end is another mad scrush and there is jostling on either side from men throwing on their clothes in a frantic dash to be rid of the pit and all its trappings. But they can't – no-one can – for even as they mingle with the rest of the population of Ashington on that fine Saturday morning, miners are betrayed by the dark rings of soot clinging to their eyelashes.

Then the bike-ride home, pretending you're Charlie Smirke on the Aga Khan's Tulyar and the bloke 50 years ahead of you is your kid brother on a carthorse. You nail him with your one good eye, and just get up to beat him by a whisker as you flash past the winning line which bisects Woolworths and the Woodhorn and Ellington Miners' Union Hall. Hordes of Saturday morning shoppers stop and turn at the sound of screeching brakes as you negotiate the Grand Hotel corner at breakneck speed. Dinner is consumed at the same crazy speed as your eyes wolf down Corsair's Nap selection gleaned from a floppy Newcastle Journal, propped up against the ubiquitous bottle of tomato sauce.

And now the footrace to the bus stop. You are the top pro, Spence of Blyth, and that scrawny kid halfway up the colliery row is Jack the Coalman, without a hope in Hell of beating you to the top of the street. And you breast the imaginary tape, stretched between backyard gate and netty door, three yards inside even-time to record the fastest time in the world that year, just as the bus pulls around the Pavilion corner.

'Pass along the bus please,' and the hard-faced conductress packs another 12 sardines into a tin that is already turning faces blue from lack of oxygen. Cigarette smoke billows around the bus, and you feel such an outcast because the one and only time you dragged on a tab it had made you retch.

'Anybody for the White Elephant?' and 60 pairs of eyes peer out of the single-decker bus windows to get a last glimpse of Ashington disappearing into the sooty blue-yonder. From now on it's foreign ground! A vile smell permeates the bus, and people stare into space, avoiding each others eyes. They needn't have worried: the bus is passing a rancid Choppington pit-heap, standing llike a big black dunce's cap on the outskirts of the dull little hamlet.

'Hartford Hall anyone?' and a miner lucky enought to have a seat, lifts his eyes from the Sporting Life. He surveys the stately building perched on the hillside and remembers the time he spent almost a year at the Hall, used as a rehabilitation centre for those injured down the pit. He had almost forgotton but his gammy leg wouldn't let him.

Countryside now, completely alien to the pitmen. On the left is the old Cramlington aerodrome, and someone remarks about the airship that used to be housed there. Old heads nod in agreement: it's proving to be a good day out already. Two more pits in quick succession: Seaton Burn and Hazelrigg. Men stub tabs out underheel and squash racing papers into jacket pockets: almost there.

'Gosforth Park anyone?' Need she have asked? 'Mind the step.' And we all jump off the bus, casting envious eyes through the windows of passing banana-coloured trolley buses at the townies sitting inside. For the lads from Ashington, there was still an uphill two furlongs to negotiate, shadowed by massive rhododendron bushes on either side. It's the last Saturday in June, and with pitmen being true men of the soil, they can appreciate the pink and purple blooms with their glossy leaves sporting 40 shades of green.

Nearly at the top of the hill now and the adrenalin begins to flow as you hear the strains of brass instruments floating down to greet you. It is the same disabled soldiers' troupe which had entertained the crowds since the end of the war. Suddenly you see them: strung right across the road like barbed-wire blocking your path. Now you are no-man's land and the same old fella with the one leg is shaking his collection box in your face as you brush past. You feel you have to contribute or bad luck will pursue you all afternoon, just as it would dog these poor sods for the rest of their lives. So your tanner goes flying into the box, and you are convinced that token gesture will keep you in credit with the Almighty for another year.

It is the turn now of a dapper bowler-hatted gentleman to harangue the milling crowd, 'Get the card! Have a gamble! Gamble till the cows come home!' You recognise him as Ki-wi the same chap who stands outside Ashington dogtrack, trying to flog his tips to rookie punters. A fresh-faced youth who cannot possibly be a pitman, digs deep into his pocket and gives Ki-wi a couple of bob in return for a small square piece of white card. 'Fresh-face' glances at the writing on it and thrusts it into his pocket lest anyone benefits from his meagre outlay. Passing the Border Minstrel pub, you suddenly remember that it is named after the horse that won the Plate in 1927, for hadn't you just read it in Corsair's column. Corsair was a man you could have faith in – except when he was tipping horses!

There are more men now, this time waving official race-cards at you: 'One pound a card! Genuine information! Money-back guarantee if not completely satisfied!' And again some fool rushes in where angels and pitmen fear to tread. Joining the queue for entrance on to the course, you jingle your pockets to make sure you can comply with the sign: 'Have correct money – no change given'. Now you are at the turnstile and you hand your three and a tanner over the counter before squeezing through the metal bars.

Yet another queue, this time for a programme. No need for a programme: you'll never get near enough to spot the colours, even if you did know whose they were. *'Beware of pickpockets'* says another sign, and a 100 hands caress their britchy-arse pockets, just in case. Another look at the watch, spots the time at a quarter to two. Still a while before the first race, so you decide to mingle. You haven't a choice really because the crowd here is so dense, moving singly is almost impossible.

A deeper than ever crush is grouped around a small table. Behind the table, a man manipulates three cards in his hands, shuffling them around before placing them face down on the table. It is yet another con: 'Find the Lady'. A *plant* in the crowd shoves a pound note on top of one of the cards and the dealer simulates an aggrieved look as he turns up the card to reveal a red queen. 'Every one a winner folks,' shouts poker-face, paying a couple of quid to his sidekick. In step the dupes with their hard-earned cash, and another swindler starts off the afternoon on the right side.

Now you push a path through to the iron rails which bar the way into the Silver Ring. You squeeze your face against an opening, looking in envy at your more prosperous compatriots who have just that little bit more elbow room. They also have access to the stone steps of the ramshackle stand which provides a better view and shelter from the prevalent north-east wind. Beyond the Silver Ring is Tattersalls, and if you could have afforded binoculars, you may just have caught a glimpse of the flamboyant Phil Bull, in his distinctive white panama hat, ambling around the Club enclosure. But here at the popular end, that's your place, just as surely as if it had been reserved for you from birth. As a Geordie lad who has worked down the pit since you left school at 15, you're a died-in-the-wool socialist – you can't afford to be owt else – yet you wonder who coined the magic phrase 'The Pitmen's Derby'. It is 1952 and probably nearer to belonging to the pitmen of Northumberland this year than it had ever done before.

For the previous 120 years, the Northumberland Plate had been run on a Wednesday. Which was fine for the landed gentry for whom each day was pretty much the same as any other. And it was OK for the tradesmen of Newcastle, as Wednesdays were traditionally early-closing. And it was great for the factory and shipyard workers who were given Race Week off as an annual holiday. But the only chance the poor Ashington miner had had to get involved with what was supposed to be *his* race, was when he put his tanner-each-way bet on with the bookie's runner, all greasy cap and shifty eyes, who could be found in any one of the 22 working men's clubs in the biggest mining village in the world. Maybe the pit-townie got Race Wednesday off, but the pitman of East Northumberland never had the chance to attend any of the mid-week runnings of the Plate. How could he? If he was in the backshift he would be at work; if he was in the nightshift he would be getting ready for work; and if he'd been in the foreshift he'd be too knackered to get out of bed!

Almost time for the first race and you rush across to the triple line of bookies shouting the odds, The tic-tac man in the white gloves is almost tying himself in a knot in an attempt to relay the prices from the Silver Ring. And the unwary punter standing out on the course suffers yet again, as he is forced to accept a price about his horse which is at least half a point less than in the other enclosures. But that's life! And you stick a ten-bob note into Honest John's flabby hand, point your finger in the direction of his board, and the bet is struck. Now it's a mad gallop to try to get some kind of vantage point, but you settle for a place near the rails, almost two furlongs from the finish.

They're off! And you strain your ears to listen to the race commentary but it's a wasted effort: you can follow your next door neighbour's sex life far easier. A minute later, the horses flash past you in a blur, but you catch sight of the No.9 on the saddlecloth of the clear leader, and that puts a few more revs on your pulse rate. You've backed a winner! You're sure of that, and you float on a No.9 cloud across to the man who out of sheer generosity, is about to quadruple your half a quid. For a moment your eyes fail to spot him and you fear the worst: he's done a runner!

But no! There he is, scowling into the faces of other successful punters as he dips into his bulging satchel, producing wads of green and white currency. At last you are face-to-face, and almost apologetically you hand across what you're convinced is a winning ticket. The bookie tears it in half and in a bored voice enquires from the clerk 'Ticket 301?' The studious fellow with long sheets of paper held together by a bulldog clip, scans his book. 'That's not a winner!' he exclaims. 'That one wasn't even shopped. I wish it had been.'

'What's your game, sonny?' asks the bookie, his fat red face growing more apoplectic by the minute. 'Trying to pull a flanker, eh! Now bugger off afore I skelp your arse!'

'But I ...' You skulk away, sure that everyone at Gosforth Park is privy to your wretched mistake. 'Wasn't even shopped!' your voice echoes in a state of disbelieving shock.

In your wandering numbness you stumble across a couple of bookies who are laying bets on the Plate – the third race on the card. Shrugging off your embarrassment, you scan the odds. With only six runners, it's the smallest Plate for 27 years. Really, you have only come to the races to back one horse: Souepi. Granted it's a stupid name for a horse, but as Corsair had pointed out, even with a 12lb penalty for winning the Ascot Gold Vase under 8st 8lb the previous week, it was still thrown in here. It was what every pitman dreams about: a handicap certainty!

The layers both had 4/5 chalked up next to Souepi. Oh no, not an odds-on shot! Another look at the Journal. Flush Royal was another to attract some attention; you could never disregard Capt Fawcus's selected. Maybe you should wait until the next race was over before you plunged. Perhaps you'd get evens for your money! You make sure no-one is watching before pulling out your wallet to check on the cash situation: you've still got ten pound notes, three half crowns and a smattering of small change. More than enough to make a killing! The ten quid is earmarked for the Plate: that is sacred, whatever happens. But what if you could make the ten into 20?

So you thrash around the bookies prior to the next race: a two-year-old maiden. You scan the boards. But what is this? You are distracted by a gaggle of noise and movement among the lines of bookies: there is a run on a horse, you know that because you've seen it all before. A swirl of men clutching crisp white fivers, ebbs and flows from one line to another, bobbing up and down for the best prices. But a price about what? You find yourself picked up and thrown around like sea-coal on the tide, and shout across to a fellow traveller 'Which horse is it?' And the reply comes drifting back to you, borne on a wave of misplaced optimism 'The favourite! It canna get beat.'

Then you are ungraciously beached in front of a flashy man in a check suit. He beckons to you with his hand 'Well, what is it?' And you wave your ten pounds at him as if to say 'A pitman's money is as good as anybody else's.' But all you can manage is 'Favourite!' And he grabs your cash and throws it contemptuously into his bag, grinning to his clerk 'An even tenner, ticket No.577.' And you suddenly realise you haven't been waving but drowning.

The loose change in your pocket rattles like Jacob Marley's chains as you stumble down to the rails to cheer on your ill-conceived wager. You wait impatiently. The horses could very well be donkeys taking part in the previous night's Donkey Derby at Brough Park, for all you know of them. You listen for titbits of information from a chap who stands nearby, neck craning, his huge hands dwarfing the opera glasses glued to piggy eyes. 'It's got no chance!' he grunts at a neighbour. 'Not a bloody snowball's chance in Hell!'

What hasn't? you mouth silently. For God's sake man, what hasn't?

'Information! That's your f...ing information for you!' And a very angry man stuffs the glasses into his pocket and stomps off.

There is no need to try to pick out the horses as they stream past you Indian fashion. And there is little need for the silent recrimination you heap upon your bowed head, trudging back to bury yourself in the animated crowd. With such an unexpected result, you wonder why the bookmakers are still scowling, but then they complain whatever wins.

You have little appetite for racing now, and as the crowds descend upon the lines of bookies to place their bets on the Plate, you join the few dozen others who have already had enough for one day, sidling anonymously through a small wooden gate out on to the path that takes you back to the bus and then eventually to the pit.

The musical ex-servicemen have thrown down their instruments and crutches, and loll about on the grass drinking ale from large pint glasses. As you pass, your eyes meet those of the man with one leg, and for an instant it is doubtful who bears the most pain. But you delve into your pocket, and setting two shillings aside for the bus, cascade the rest of your silver coins into the empty collection box.

That'll do for next year!

Rounding the Final Bend

The year of 1950 was not a good one for racing. As the lifestyle of the racing public improved with more money to spend and more consumer goods being made available, so the attendances at racetracks fell by up to 15 per cent. Racecourse executives began to have sleepless nights as they pondered on ways to draw the public back to their tracks.

Yet for Gosforth, the 1950s was a vintage era for the Northumberland Plate with some magical characters from the turf appearing regularly at the Gosforth Park meetings. Young jockeys were coming to the fore: Lester Piggott, Jimmy Lindley, Joe Mercer and the ever-popular Jimmy Etherington. Incredibly this quartet were still looked upon as apprentices in 1954 even though they had ridden dozens of winners: Piggott an Epsom Derby included.

The terms of an apprenticeship contract: 'binds him to a licensed trainer for a term of not less than three years'. So a prolific rider such as Mercer was an apprentice without a weight allowance.

One up and coming young lad who was able to claim an allowance in the early 50s was Edward Hide. Born in 1937, son of a Ludlow trainer, Eddie went to the scale at a little less than 6st 7lb. In 1956 Hide had 368 rides gaining 43 victories, many for Syd Mercer of Birmingham who put the lad up whenever he could obtain his services.

Eddie had the right temperament, was a natural horseman with the knack of never getting flustered or over-anxious when in a tight squeeze. But he snapped up every opportunity, such as when Bill Dutton the Malton trainer utilised Hide's expertise, and the pair were successful in the Plate with Great Rock in 1957. Hide needed a cool head that day when a controversial melee at the first bend left seven horses without jockeys as they crashed to the ground. Dutton himself was an able horseman as he had shown by winning the Grand National on Tipperary Tim. Eddie Hide continued to enjoy a successful riding career, highlighted by a 1973 Derby win on Morston.

Joe Mercer was still considered to be an apprentice when he rode Nick La Rocca to win the 1953 Plate. By sheer coincidence his mount and the winner from the previous year Souepi, ran a deadheat in the Doncaster Cup. By Epigram, Souepi was owned jointly by his trainer George Digby and Mohammed Bey Sultan. This unlikely duo had come together when Digby was riding in Egypt where he was champion jockey for 14 years. Souepi never ran as a two-year-old and when he did race at three his jockey was of the opinion that he would never get beyond six furlongs.

Running uplaced in all seven starts at three, it wasn't till Souepi was four that his talent as a stayer became apparent. As well as the Plate he won the Ascot Gold Vase, the Goodwood Cup and the Gold Cup. As Bert Packham dismounted the odds-on winner he said: 'I last came up here 20 years ago, but the horse I was due to ride didn't run. So this is my very first mount at Newcastle!' Such was the poor esteem in which stayers in this country were held, Souepi was allowed to be exported to Chile for a paltry 2,300 guineas.

The small field that turned out that day was blamed on the presence of Souepi by trainers unwilling to pit their charges against this seemingly 'good thing' carrying only 7st 6lbs. This was unfortunate, because 1952 had been chosen as the year to move the traditional Plate Wednesday to a Saturday. When questioned afterwards, clerk of the course Randolph Gibson professed himself highly satisfied: 'Holding the Northumberland Plate on a Saturday for the first time in 120 years was an experiment sufficiently successful to warrant its continuation. It is intended to adhere to Saturday, and it has already been allocated by the Jockey Club who are definitely in favour. So far as we are concerned, it has proved a success. I was among the crowd and they were very pleased.'

Referring to trainer Charlie Elsey's comment that it should revert to a Wednesday because it now clashed with Doncaster, Gibson retorted: 'Let Doncaster take Tuesday and Wednesday, and give someone else a chance! We had 40,000 here today and it would have been more if the Plate field hadn't cut up so badly! I personally was quite satisfied.'

Joe Mercer also won the big Newcastle race on Master of Arts for Jakie Astor and Jack Colling in 1958, in one of the biggest fields ever to take part in the Pitmen's Derby. Twenty-one runners lined up that day and unlike the old Town Moor days, 21 runners completed the race.

Racecourse attendances throughout the country rose in 1955 due partly to an industrial dispute among journalists which meant that all national newspapers were off the street for over a month, hence no information was available on runners and riders. Another severe inconvenience that year was a railwaymen's strike which resulted in a state of emergency being declared by the Queen. Because of this Royal Ascot took place *after* the Plate meeting and not before it.

Lester Piggott, blazed his way into the Pitmen's Derby history by guiding Little Cloud home that year. Willie Nevett and other veteran riders were well aware of the young tearaway's fiery record – he had been suspended for six months the previous year – and they decided to give 18-year-old Lester a hard time.

Said Willie 'He wasn't much more than a slip of a kid but three or four of the lads gave him the works. And Lester was nearly down three times but he just picked up the horse and went on to win as though nothing had happened.'

It was indirectly through Sir Gordon Richards that Lester Piggott had the mount on Little Cloud. Richards had been Noel Murless's stable jockey for a number of years before having a crashing fall at Sandown in July of 1954, shortly after winning his one and only Plate at Gosforth on Friseur.

Because of the severe pelvic injury sustained, Sir Gordon who had become the Turf's first knight the previous year, was forced to retire from riding. This left Murless without a jockey, and he tried to get Willie Snaith, Scobie Breasley and

Mannie Mercer to join him before settling for the precocious talents of young Lester.

Noel Murless was born in Cheshire in 1910. His first job was as a jump jockey attached to the stables of Frank Hartigan and later his brother Hubert. When Murless set up on his own in Yorkshire he very quickly made a name for himself, and on the retirement of Fred Darling moved into the successful Beckhampton stables. This move was only temporary and Murless eventually settled at Newmarket. Said Lester Piggott of Noel Murless who was responsible for training a hat-trick of Plate winners in 1954/5/6: 'His hat was one of the oldest I have ever seen. I am sure someone had broken it in for him'.

Capt Elsey had a capable lad in Don Morris who was yet another to win the Plate while still officially an apprentice in 1959. He drove 100–7 outsider Cannabiere up on the rails to win for A Barclay, the Penrith trainer, carrying a mere 7st 11lb. At six years of age Cannabiere was the oldest horse to win since Elsey's 1933 winner Leonard. This record was smashed when Treasure Hunter won in 1987 at the ripe old age of eight.

Lester Piggott had less than happy memories of the 1961 Plate when he was dumped on his backside as top-weight Sunny Way came down shortly before entering the straight. Winner that day was Utrillo, a chance ride for young D Cullen. Ron Hutchison had been booked but backed out at the last minute to send Utrillo's odds spiralling to 20–1.

The *Newcastle Journal* front page set the scene that morning on the last Saturday in June, 1961: 'With the weather forecast of a fine and sunny 72 degrees, High Gosforth Park is surely now at its very best. The famous rhododendrons are in full colour and the course has never looked so good. Thousands of pounds have been spent in brightening up the Park for the Queen Mother who unfortunately will not be attending because of a foot injury. Sixteen million gallons of water have been sprinkled on the course where cloth caps will mingle with high hats as the clock treads slowly to the big moment at 3.40 pm.'

A Willie Stephenson protege, young Irishman Des Cullen got Utrillo home for Bill O'Gorman by a neck and the same from Brocade Slipper and Avon's Pride. 'That's the first big race I've won,' said young Des, and his tutor Stephenson endorsed the young lad's future 'He has been with me for five years, and he is staying with me.'

The Northumberland Plate has enjoyed Royal connections since 1901 when the Duke of Clarence, eldest son of Edward VII, came up to see his Reminiscence win. And in 1959 the Princess Royal was present to see her All Serene run unplaced behind Cannabiere. The Queen Mother blessed the occasion in 1962 on the 100th anniversary of the Blaydon Races song. It was hoped she would see the Queen's colours carried to victory by Optimistic, only to be short-headed by Geoff Littlewood on Bordone, for another great northern institution Buster Fenningworth of Richmond. The Queen had a runner in the Durham Plate half an hour earlier, but Hasty Gold ridden by D W Morris as was Optimistic, also failed to win for Her Majesty.

The Queen Mother was in the North-East for four days, staying at Alnwick Castle as a guest of the Duke of Northumberland. On the Sunday she sailed to the Farne Islands and on the following day was one of a vast record crowd visiting the Royal Agricultural Show on Newcastle's Town Moor: the last Show before it was permanently sited at Stoneleigh in Warwickshire.

Peter Robinson was another young rider to excel when topping the apprentice league in 1956 with 46 winners. Based initially with Harry Wragg, young Peter proved himself to be a good horseman, showing patience and judgement of pace when he got the Farnham Maxwell-trained Horse Radish home in the 1963 Plate. Peter became a trainer in 1969. He was responsible for a good old-fashioned gamble when his Prince de Galles was backed down to 5–2 favourite in a field of 26 for the Cambridgeshire, and the three-year-old romped home by an easy four lengths. The Robinson name is still carried on by his son Philip who is an outstanding young rider.

Many good horses were redirected to Newcastle when Royal Ascot was abandoned in 1964. Newcastle's gain was Ascot's loss as owners missed out on £75,000 in prizes. Commented the Duke of Norfolk 'We have lost heavily'. Major Priestman who lived at Slaley Mill near Hexham was expected to go close in the Plate on his home course, and his Outcrop was a warm favourite. But the 22,500 crowd saw Peter Piper romp home by five lengths in the hands of Jock Wilson in a field which included two former Plate winners Utrillo and Horse Radish. Ron Mason, the winning trainer, was a former speedway rider and had scored an impressive three out of three with his runners at Newcastle. Outcrop finished in the rear as did that fine stayer Grey of Falloden. At the end of the meeting Randolph Gibson professed himself well pleased with the 37,000 turn out for the three days.

Plate Winners in the 1960s

Date	winner	owner	trainer	jockey	SP
1960	New Brig	J Kennedy	G Boyd	N Stirk	10–1
1961	Utrillo	J Gerber	W O'Gorman	D Cullen	100–7
1962	Bordone	A Grant	G Fen'worth	G Littlewood	100–7
1963	Horse Radish	N Wachman	F Maxwell	P Robinson	8–1
1964	Peter Piper	Mrs V Phillips	R Mason	J Wilson	28–1
1965	Cagirama	Mrs S Carson	G Boyd	N McIntosh	9–1
1966	Sweet Story	Duke of Roxburghe	R Peacock	J Etherington	100–7
1967	Piaco	Mrs O Watney	G Barling	M Thomas	100–30
1968	Amateur	Lord Derby	B V Cutsem	W Carson	100–9
1969	Even Say	S Terry	R Jarvis	F Durr	6–1

The Betting and Gaming Act of 1960 altered the betting habits of a whole nation of stay-at-home punters. Up till then their only recourse to a wager was with the bookie's runners who hung around almost every pub, club and corner-end in the land. Most of them did very good business and were a thorn in the side of local bobbies who tried – sometimes not all that rigorously – to move them along. It is not at all certain that the people who frequented the betting shops as they opened in 1961 did much to alter attendances at racecourses as betting shop punters were not necessarily the type to go racing.

Another innovation at the time was the introduction of the patrol film camera which provided head-on views of a race within a few minutes of its completion. It eased the tasks of the much-maligned stewards and resulted in far less non-triers using the track as a warm-up for richer pickings.

The year of 1962 sparked off yet another fire at Gosforth Park which devastated Randolph Gibson as much as it did the grandstand, and he left the supervision of the new complex in the capable hands of a new clerk of the course: A C (Freddie) Newton.

A popular winner in 1966 for senior Jockey Club steward the Duke of Roxburghe, was Sweet Story. Jockey Jimmy Etherington was born in 1934 in Leicester and began riding when he was nine years old. His father had always been interested in riding and it was that which started him off. He did a bit of show-jumping first of all and when he was 16 went as an apprentice to Ernie Davey at Malton. Jimmy's first winner was a horse called Xebec at Bogside in 1951. Top apprentice by a long way that year was Lester Piggott with over 80 winners, and Jimmy and Joe Mercer finished joint second with 26 apiece.

'First trainer I went to as a fully-fledged rider was Billy Bellerby at Malton,' said Jimmy. 'Shortly after that I had two retainers, one with the Duke of Roxburghe and the other for Peter Easterby. I was with the Duke for five years and always got on well with him. He was a smashing fella, always seemed a bit of a bluff character, quite formidable, but his bark was worse than his bite. Easterby was great to ride for! He never gave any instructions, just let you get on with it. It ended up I was with him for 14 years.

'Sweet Story was a horse I'd ridden for the Duke and Dick Peacock in 1965 and it had won about three times before they ran it in the Plate. He was a character who hated the stalls and always jumped out very slowly. But as it happened they didn't use stalls that particular year at Newcastle.

'I can remember it had been a very wet year in 1966 and the ground had got very boggy. So I took an outside position right from the off to look for the better ground and at one time I must have been racing half way across the track. But the horse ran on very well and I got a good run up the rails to win quite cleverly in the end by a length.

'There was very little money for the winner, but the stable was hopeful. The one sad thing was that the Duke who had his heart set on winning the Northumberland Plate, for some reason couldn't get along that day to see his horse win. That was the first big race win for Sweet Story but the following year he won the Yorkshire Cup and the Lutine Stakes at Ascot.

'Newcastle has always been a lucky track for me both as a jockey and a trainer. I retired from riding when I was 35 because of weight problems, and took over a

61

stable at Malton. The Geordie crowd are always very generous and I look upon Gosforth Park as my favourite course.'

Sweet Story was aimed at the Plate the following year but had to give second best to the brilliant but obstinate Piaco owned by Mrs O Watney. The Geoff Barling-trained Piaco only ran a couple of times at two, and was such a cuss of an animal that he was gelded. Benefits gained from the operation included the Doncaster Cup and the Kenneth Robertson Stakes at Sandown. Piaco declined two Ascot engagements to run at Newcastle where he was ridden by M Thomas. L G Brown had the mount this time on Sweet Story, and must have thought he'd made it two in a row for the Duke of Roxburghe's horse when he led with less than 50 yards to go. 'I had a good run throughout,' said Brown, 'and when I took the lead I felt as if I was sure to win until I saw Taffy and Piaco, then I wished the winning post to come quickly.' The Queen's Gaulois finished a dismal eleventh of 13 runners.

A year later it was the turn of wee Willie Carson to steer Lord Derby's Amateur home for the young lad's biggest success of his career. Carson, a cheerful Scot, was first apprenticed to Gerald Armstrong and then to Sam Armstrong. The turning point in Willie's career came in 1967 when he was picked by Bernard Van Cutsem to be Lord Derby's stable jockey: the connections responsible for Amateur.

One of the greatest personalities in racing to win the Northumberland Plate was Harry Dalmeny Primrose, otherwise known as the 6th Earl of Rosebery, owner of the 1973 winner Tom Cribb. His father was the only man to have won the Epsom Derby while still a Prime Minister. At Eton, Dalmeny was an outstanding athlete and also captained the Surrey Cricket Eleven. It was he who gave the great Jack Hobbs his first county cap.

During the First World War he was badly wounded but still managed to pick up the DSO, the MC and the Legion of Honour. He flirted for a time with politics as the Liberal MP for Mid Lothian, but it was in the field of racing that Lord Rosebery is to be remembered. Following on from his father, he continued a close association with Jack Jarvis which resulted in the Classic wins of Blue Peter and Ocean Swell. Lord Rosebery died at the age of 92 in 1974.

David Robinson was another racing legend to own a Plate winner: Grey God in 1975. Robinson was a self-made millionaire who made his fortune from the radio and television business. He began making inroads into the world of racing in the 1940s but proved quite difficult to please when it came to finding trainers for his horses. In 1962 he bought the Carlburg stables at Newmarket and installed Bruce Hobbs to oversee his rapidly expanding racing empire. Hobbs who trained the 1973 Plate winner Tom Cribb had at one time been a jockey over the sticks, winning the Grand National on the tiny Battleship in 1938.

Hobbs turned out more than a few winners for Robinson but was still replaced by Jimmy Thompson of Beverley. Thompson went the same way as Hobbs and by 1968 the Robinson dynasty of over 70 horses was spread between Michael Jarvis and Paul Davey. Indeed it was Jarvis who trained Grey God and four years later Totowah to give Lady Beaverbrook her first Plate win.

Bruce Raymond was only 17 when he rode his first winner at Birmingham in 1962. Bruce's guv'nor Willie Stephenson said of him 'I think he will reach the top; he's a very good rider indeed.' Bruce justified Stephenson's optimism when he captured the two Pitmen's Derbys on Grey God and Totowah.

Most Recent Plate Winners

	winner	*owner*	*trainer*	*jockey*	*SP*
1970	Philoctetes	P Bull	S Ingham	P Eddery	20–1
1971	Tartar Prince	J Parker	T Waugh	J Higgins	5–1
1972	Scoria	J Lang	C Crossley	R Smyth	17–2
1973	Tom Cribb	Lord Rosebery	B Hobbs	B Jago	11–1
1974	Attivo	Peter O'Sullevan	C Mitchell	R Wernham	7–4
1975	Grey God	David Robinson	M Jarvis	B Raymond	8–1
1976	Philominski	S Hallam	W Marshall	R Marshall	20–1
1977	Tug of War	Mrs Y Perry	D Whelan	B Rouse	16–1
1978	Tug of War	Mrs Y Perry	D Whelan	B Rouse	11–2
1979	Totowah	Lady Beaverbrook	M Jarvis	B Raymond	5–1
1980	Mons Beau	Mr M Vine	E Beeson	S Salmon	40–1
1981	Dawn Johnny	Sir Gdn White	M Stoute	M Birch	5–1
1982	*Course waterlogged*				
1983	Weaver's Pin	Mrs M Francis	M D Francis	P Eddery	20–1
1984	Karadar	H H Aga Khan	M Stoute	A Kimberley	10–1
1985	Trade Line	M D Scott	R Sheather	T Williams	7–2
1986	Sneak Preview	Mrs C E Gross	H Candy	S Whitworth	4–1
1987	Treasure Hunter	J Fitzgerald	J Fitzgerald	L Charnock	20–1
1988	Stavordale	Mrs Thom' Jones	Thom' Jones	M Roberts	9–4
1989	Orpheus	Sheikh Mohammed	G Harwood	R Fox	4–1

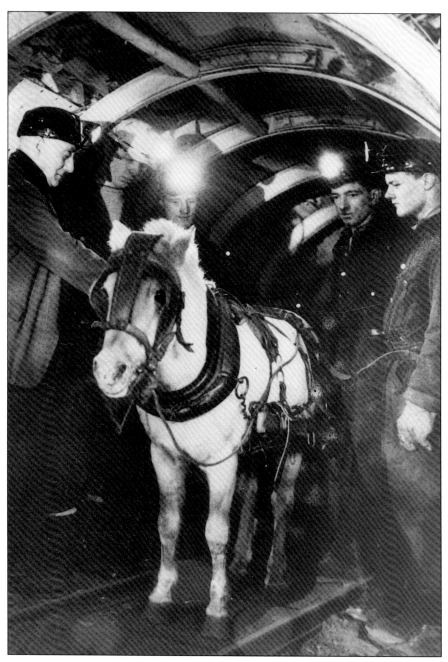

*Pit ponies were used extensively in Northumberland in low and narrow workings. They were bred in Galloway and became known as **Gallowas**.*

No champers for Lester as he walks back after being dumped by Sunny Way in 1961.

The Queen Mother congratulates Geoff Littlewood who won on Bordone in 1962 for Buster Fenningworth.

Whitehall 3141

CLARENCE HOUSE
S.W.1

5th July, 1962

Dear Dick,

I am writing at the bidding of Queen Elizabeth The Queen Mother to tell you how very greatly Her Majesty enjoyed her visit to Gosforth Park, and how grateful Her Majesty is for your kindness and hospitality.

Everything that you had laid on was quite excellent and it was a wonderfully successful after-noon. It could only have been more perfect if 'Harvest Gold' and 'Optimistic' had both triumphed, but the Racecourse could not be blamed for that omission. However, I am certain that their defeat will not discourage Queen Elizabeth from coming again on some future occasion.

May I also thank you most sincerely on behalf of Lady Hambleden and myself for all your generous hospitality, which we greatly appreciated.

Finally, I wonder if you would be good enough to let Mr. Gibson know how delighted Her Majesty was with all his arrangements.

Yours ever,

Martin Gilliat.

Lieutenant-Colonel R.I.G. Taylor, DSO.

Letter from the Queen Mother's Equerry to the Course Chairman, Col Dick Taylor.

Norman Stirk dismounts from New Brig in 1960 (above).
Horse Radish won in 1963 when ridden by Peter Robinson (below left) and trained by
Farnham Maxwell (below right).

(Above) Utrillo and Des Cullen won the 1961 Plate.
(Below) Jock Wilson got Peter Piper home by an easy five lengths in 1964 at 28–1.

Sweet Story wins in 1966 (above) for the 9th Duke of Roxburghe who was also a senior steward (below left). Trainer, Dick Peacock (below right).

Jimmy Etherington, Sweet Story's jockey, now training at Malton, counts Gosforth Park as his favourite course.

Piaco won the big prize for Mrs O V Watney in 1967 (above). Alec Marsh was the official starter that day (left).

Philoctetes wins – whichever way you look at it (above). Maginot Line (no.15) was second; Tantivy (no.2) was third; with St Patrick's Blue (no.4) fourth (below).

MR
DAVID
ROBINSON

Phil Bull receives the 1970 Plate from Lord Howard de Walden as Freddie Newton stands front right (above). Bruce Raymond (below) rode two Plate winners, including Grey God for millionaire, David Robinson.

The versatile Attivo wins for Peter O'Sullevan, from both angles, in 1974.

Tug of War beats Sea Pigeon in 1977 ... and won the following year as well.

Clerks of the Course

A C (Freddie) Newton, now officiating at Ripon, first joined the Gosforth Park team in April 1962. Randolph Gibson, who had been clerk of the course since just after the war, was taken ill, and Freddie, already under contract to two other courses, was to oversee the day-to-day running of affairs until he was able to give a full-time commitment at Gosforth in 1965. He later took on the role of Managing Director in 1969.

He recalls: 'Tattersalls Stand was burnt down in December 1962, and the Levy Board made funds available to rebuild the stand and construct a new Members Stand on the Paddock Lawn. When they were officially opened in April 1965 they were welcomed as amongst the best race course developments at that time. In the years that followed, many of the buildings were modernised and the course improved.

'The peak years of attendance were in my early days with crowds of over 20,000 on Plate Days and Bank Holidays. But the advent of betting shops in 1962 reduced our attendance by up to 40 per cent. This was common to all racecourses, and the vast crowds that came then were never seen again except at one or two of the top courses.

'In those days you had the great characters of racing like Major L B Holliday who operated one of the largest private stables in Britain – apart from the Aga Khan family there was no Arab influence; David Robinson also had a stable of over 100 horses. The generation of northern flat trainers in my initial days at High Gosforth Park: Sam Hall, Harry Peacock, Charlie Elsey and Buster Fenningworth have all passed on. Geoffrey Barling nearly always had runners at Newcastle, and Noel Murless and Bernard Van Cutsem were frequent visitors. The National Hunt trainers seem to stay better: Neville Crump, Arthur Stephenson and Ken Oliver were the great supporters when I first arrived, and of those three only Neville has recently retired.

'For many years the Duke of Roxburghe was a senior steward at Newcastle – his favourite course – and he didn't suffer fools gladly! He was a brilliant reader of a race, and won the Northumberland Plate with Sweet Story in 1966. In fact, he only failed by a head to win it the next year with the same horse. Col Dick Taylor was Chairman of the High Gosforth Park Company from 1957 to 1982 and he was a great leader. I could not have done what I did without his unfailing support and guidance.

'The Queen Mother came twice to Newcastle when I was there, the first being in 1962 when she displayed great sportsmanship at the presentation even though Her Majesty's Optimism had only been beaten by a short-head. Her second visit was in 1973 when the Whitbread Gold Cup was run at Newcastle. In my opinion, the greatest achievement in the Plate when I was as Gosforth must be the wins in successive years of Tug of War in 1977/78 under weights of 8st 10lbs and 9st 2 lbs respectively.

My appointment was different in 1965 inasmuch as I was the first manager of the course living on the High Gosforth Park Estate. My brief was to expand racing. In 1962 there were only eight days Flat and four days National Hunt racing. In 1985 when I left, there were 25 meetings (12 Flat, 13 National Hunt). In addition, I also expanded the Estate activities. In 1965 we received a rent from the Northumberland Golf Club, a small income from functions in the racecourse stands, and minor sums of money for letting land and grazing. My appointment coincided with the leasing of the premises to Scottish and Newcastle Breweries for functions in between race meetings and also as racecourse caterers. The function trade was very successful. In 1966, a golf driving range was introduced and subsequently an 18-hole golf course was constructed. A caravan camp for tourists was established and a garden centre was set up in the nursery gardens. All of these enterprises contributed substantially to funds and were of great assistance to the Company in times of depression in the economy. Apart from these commercial enterprises there is a permanent Boys Scouts Camp in the Park, a 150-acre Nature Reserve and 300 acres of woodland which were felled when necessary and replanted.

'Nevertheless, racing was and will, I trust, remain the overwhelming major enterprise at Gosforth. Many good races have been introduced over the last 25 years: the Fighting Fifth Hurdle, Beeswing Stakes etc. And other races have developed: the Eider Chase and Gosforth Park Cup, and this must be an ongoing process. The policies of the Turf Association have NOT been helpful to Newcastle and other northern courses! Large southern meetings are allowed to clash now with key northern fixtures, and it goes without saying that most of the 'goodies' are reserved for the South. This is probably fair enough given the dearth of good horses trained in the North, but a fairer distribution of major races to northern courses might have been an encouragement to owners to put better class horses in training in the North.'

Present incumbent of what could never be called *the best job in the world* is David Parmley who arrived in the North-East from Lancashire in 1987. Although he has always been a keen racing enthusiast it was as a chartered accountant that he was trained. 'Knowing anything about horses is a definite liability as far as being clerk of the course is concerned,' he admits.

He is in for a rough ride following on from Freddie Newton and Randolph Gibson, both of whom became institutions in their own right during their lengthy stays at the course. David set about this daunting task by inaugurating a communication link between the course and the media, for he soon realised that a friendly press is a good ally in keeping the public informed.

And all this talk of 'Gosforth Park going under' ... is this just a scare-mongering tactic on his part? 'Not at all,' he says. 'Unless our proposed new development goes ahead it is impossible to look into the future with any degree of certainty. Racing at Newcastle is not profitable and High Gosforth Park Plc have subsidised the sport for many years with income derived from activities elsewhere on the Estate.

Unfortunately there is now insufficient other income to generate profits. To combat this we have planned an imaginative development scheme which will secure Tyneside's future as far as racing is concerned. This will incorporate high-quality housing, discreetly situated and blending in completely with the rest of the Park. It is a small price to pay for a guaranteed stream of income which will be used to re-establish Newcastle as a premier racecourse.

'Usually preparations for the Plate begin at least 12 months in advance. If we can satisfy customers on one Plate Day then they will come back the following year. One of the innovations we have set up is the tented village. It is now very popular and we are able to let everthing we erect. All the chalets are on the Club lawn, affording a full view of all the proceedings. Larger marquees are still sited in the centre of the course. Considerable co-ordination is required between caterers, marquee operators and various contractors who provide television, electrical and water connections so that a full closed-circuit television and tote service can be provided for the tented village.

'If we can get some decent weather then we can normally expect about 15,000 racegoers on Plate Day. It is the most valuable two-mile handicap in Britain, and is, therefore, very popular with owners and trainers. Race conditions are published in the February and an owner has to make his mind up by the end of May. Declarations are five days before the race and will cost a £500 entry fee.

'The state of the going is always uppermost in a trainer's mind, especially nowadays when we seem to get so little rain, and a report is given six days in advance of the race. That gives connections one clear day to make up their minds. Additional going reports are given at the two-day and 24-hours stage. Each of these reports requires a course inspection which involves a walk around the course testing the ground with a stick.

'Come the big day, I'm usually on the go at half past six! First there's the course inspection, then a check to see if the race cards have arrived – that's always a heart-stopping moment: once a race was missed out, but luckily it only involved a few cards and we were able to withdraw those. The state of the going has to be telephoned to various people and I usually give a radio interview. By then I'm dying for a cuppa so I dash over to the house and get changed in between sips of tea.

'Now the foreman will be on site and we walk the course together making any last-minute adjustments to things like advertising hoardings. The casual staff will then be starting to arrive and will need to be briefed as will the commissionaires, stewards, Jockey Club officials and the Police and security staff.

'We had a nightmare in 1988 when we received a phone call from Newmarket saying that someone had made a threat to kill Greville Starkey and his horse Zero Watt. What had happened was that two men and a girl, speaking in Spanish, had been overheard by someone in a Leeds cafe who also spoke Spanish, discussing ways of disposing of Starkey. A gun lay under the table wrapped in a black bin-liner. Yes, I know it sounds all too far fetched! But this informant had rung up

Newmarket thinking Starkey was riding there, and a Newmarket official had relayed the message on to me.

'Well, what could I do? I daren't NOT believe it. Luckily the Chief Constable was at the course for lunch and he took over. Plain-clothed CID men toting guns were drafted in and a full-scale major alert was put into operation – one of them even borrowed my binoculars! We approached Greville Starkey, briefed him and gave him the option of dropping out if he wanted. But he treated the whole thing very lightly and got on with his job. We had to take it all seriously because Starkey had been involved in the disqualification of Royal Gait only days before in the Ascot Gold Cup. Starkey's Sadeem had been awarded the race on Royal Gait losing the race in the stewards' box. You see, Royal Gait had Spanish connections, so there was just a chance ...

'From all that you can see that the clerk of the course is responsible for *anything and everything* on Plate Day, or any other day for that matter!'

A Furlong to Go

Of today's top-notch riders, perhaps the best young jockey to come and win the Plate was Pat Eddery in 1970 when he had the mount on Philoctetes owned by northern racing stalwart Phil Bull and trained by Staff Ingham. The bearded Bull, one-time schoolmaster who named most of his horses after heroes in Greek mythology, must have worked a piece of sorcery with the horse, for with three zeros beside its name in the form book, it won completely unfancied at 20–1; exactly the same price as Eddery's subsequent 1983 winner, Weaver's Pin. The young lad was lucky to be on the mount at all! At Chepstow the night before he had been stood down for seven days after being charged with dangerous riding with resulted in D Yates being thrown from his horse. Eddery, whose suspension was to take effect after the Plate meeting, found himself behind a wall of horses with less than 100 yards to go; it was here that the Duke of Roxburghe's Maginot Line, ridden by Clive Eccleston, broke down allowing sufficient room for Philoctetes to squeeze through. A distraught Eccleston said later 'My horse was running on for me and I am sure he would have won'. As it was, Maginot Line was only beaten a length with Tantivy and the Queen's St Patrick's Blue a couple of short-heads away.

Phil Bull, who died earlier this year, was taken aback by his horse's victory: 'This is a surprise result – I fancied Tantivy!' Bull began to get noticed in racing circles during the Second World War. A radical thinker, his views on racing were not always welcomed by the 'old guard' but he has without doubt left a legacy as breeder, owner and inventor of the 'Timeform' system which sets him apart as one of the brightest and most enlightened men in twentieth century Turf history.

Trainer of Philoctetes, Staff Ingham was apprenticed to Stanley Wootton who won the 1910 Plate on Elizabetta. In 1925 as a young boy he won the Royal Hunt Cup, and was a highly respected jockey over hurdles in the 30s. Just after taking out a trainer's licence, the Second World War began and he joined the RAF rising to the rank of Squadron Leader. After the war he took a stable at Epsom and was responsible for some very big coups both on the Flat and over the sticks. Ingham died in 1977, the same year as that fine Yorkshire trainer of stayers, Sam Hall.

The well-backed Tartar Prince was given the Newcastle prize on a 'plate' in 1971 when the South African jockey John Gorton riding Stowaway eased his mount and began looking for danger over his right shoulder. He completely failed to spot John Higgins on Tartar Prince coming up on his inside, and by the time Gorton realised what was happening it was too late.

In 1974 it was that great little horse Attivo (nicknamed Percy) owned by broadcasting personality Peter O'Sullevan, who became the first horse since Elizabetta to complete the Chester Cup/Northumberland Plate double in the same year. Unfortunately Peter was *Calling the Horses* in the Irish Sweeps Derby that day and the only view he had of Attivo winning was through a very small spluttering black and white monitor placed beside him in the commentary box.

He told me: 'I sat there watching the race at Newcastle on the box, and had this marvellous feeling when Attivo passed the post in front. Somehow I got on with my job, but someone told me later that there had been a stewards' enquiry called at Newcastle. Just then all hell was let loose at The Curragh when it was announced over the tannoy that the place had to be evacuated because of a bomb-scare! I just sat there thinking to myself: I'm going to be blown up and I'll not even know if Attivo has survived an objection.'

Luckily for Peter the controversy had nothing to do with the 7–4 winner, and the versatile Attivo who had already won the Daily Express Triumph Hurdle at Cheltenham the same year, notched up yet another victory in a remarkable sequence of wins. On the strength of Percy's string of successes, Peter was voted by his fellow writers as 'Owner of the Year' prompting him to reply in verse:

> *An accolade from such a source*
> *Would turn the head of any horse.*
> *(For, of course, I realise*
> *It was Attivo won the prize.)*

Geordie racegoers were treated to the best between 1977 and 1980 when the ever-popular Sea Pigeon ran in four consecutive Plates. Carrying mountains of weight, Pat Muldoon's gallant stayer finished second behind Tug of War in '77 and fourth on the other three occasions.

Twice-winning Northumberland Plate trainer in the 80s with Dawn Johnny and Karadar, Michael Stoute almost became a BBC racing commentator in 1965 when beaten in a photo-finish with Julian Wilson in the trial race to partner 'old hand' O'Sullevan.

The High Gosforth Park Chairman, Roy Baker, nearly kept the Tyneside prize at home in 1983, but his Prince Santiago had to give best to Pat Eddery and Weaver's Pin. Third that day was the Aga Khan's Karadar who came back the next year to achieve a fine weight-carrying feat in humping 9st 10lb to victory around the stiff two-miles.

Another Royal horse to compete in the Pitmen's Derby was the Queen's Insular who could only finish fifth behind Trade Line and the fast-finishing favourite Nestor, in the 1985 Brown Ale Plate. An American owner's name went on the Roll of Honour the following year when Sneak Preview justified his favouritism.

The 1987 winner, Treasure Hunter, produced mixed feelings for various people. Peter Illingworth, headteacher at Newcastle's Heaton Manor School, won £2,488 on a Tote dual forecast with a £2 bet on Treasure Hunter (20–1) and Stavordale (11–1). 'I included Stavordale in my forecast because I read what Doug Moscrop (Underhand of the Journal) had to say.'

Not so happy were Adam and Mary Robson, former owners of the winner, who had given Treasure Hunter away to his trainer Jimmy Fitzgerald at the beginning of the season. The last time the horse had carried Mrs Robson's colours was in the 1986 Plate when Treasure Hunter could do no better than finish tenth.

The ground was too firm for him last year,' said Adam Robson. 'We are delighted that he won this year, but it's hard to accept he has.' For Jimmy Fitzgerald this was his lucky day! The nearest he had come prior to this was when he received place money with Special Vintage and Vicomte. Sneak Preview winner the previous year, trailed in last but one. And second horse home Stavordale, came back the following year to win in a driving finish for Michael Roberts.

Last year's prize money was the highest ever with £50,000 added, but as so often happens nowadays the spoils went to the Ruler of Dubai's number-three-son, Sheik Mohammed (Geordie Ridley would have had problems with that one) and a southern trainer Guy Harwood, who told me 'I think our feeling about the Northumberland Plate is that it is an extremely valuable handicap which is very attractive to all staying handicappers in the country.

'It is always one of the races we are trying to lay our horses out for at the start of the season and indeed this was the case with Orpheus. We had also tried to win the race the year before with Zero Watt who was unfortunately beaten a short head.'

Little wonder that Orpheus started at 4–1 joint favourite: he was the sole survivor of Harwood's original list of ten entries. The other joint favourite was Cold Marble ridden by Franco Vittori and trained at Newmarket by newcomer William Haggas. 'Having experienced the unique atmosphere of the Pitmen's Derby on Tyneside the year before when Cold Marble won the Coral Line Handicap,' he said, 'I decided there and then to try and win the Plate. I had laid him out for the race because he was a true two-miler.'

High drama and High Gosforth Park have always gone hand-in-hand, and the 1989 Northumberland Plate witnessed by a crowd of 13,000 was full of incident. Bottom-weight Metannee slipped up on a bend after six furlongs, and subsequently interfered with Cold Marble, Jinga and the eventual second Ala Hounak; in the melee, top-weight Mr Pintips was brought down. As Orpheus became the first three-year-old to win since Joe Chamberlain in 1900, unlucky trainer Haggas reported Cold Marble had an injured hock, almost certainly caused in the incident. Winning jockey, Richard Fox, remembered the race this way: 'With only 7st 7lb on his back I had to strike early! I took a peep over my shoulder two furlongs from home, saw no danger, and thought: that's a job well done!'

And as the Northumberland Plate strides majestically into the last decade of this twentieth century, we can only echo the same sentiments of gratitude to those who have laboured before us to give the North-East its greatest living sporting legacy: *that's a job well done!'*

Plate Winners at a Glance

Date	Winner	Date	Winner	Date	Winner
1833	Tomboy	1882	Victor Emanuel	1935	Doreen Jane
1834	Fanny	1883	Barcaldine	1936	Coup de Roi
1835	Satan	1884	Lawminster	1937	Nectar II
1836	Cyprian	1885	Blue Grass	1938	Union Jack
1837	Wedge	1886	Stoneclink	1939	Oracion
1838	St Bennet	1887	Exmoor	1946	Gusty
1839	St Bennet	1888	Matin Bell	1947	Culrain
1840	Herman Platoff	1889	Drizzle	1948	Pappatea
1841	Calypso	1890	Houndsditch	1949	Fol Ami
1842	Heslington	1891	Queen's Birthday	1950	Light Cavalry
1843	Mosstrooper	1892	Newcourt	1951	Sycomore II
1844	The Era	1893	Seaton Delaval	1952	Souepi
1845	Inheritress	1894	Newcourt	1953	Nick La Rocca
1846	Dolo	1895	The Docker	1954	Friseur
1847	Ervx	1896	Dare Devil	1955	Little Cloud
1848	Chanticleer	1897	Bradwardine	1956	Jardiniere
1849	John Crosser	1898	King Crow	1957	Great Rock
1850	Elthiron	1899	Sherburn	1958	Master of Arts
1851	Neasham	1900	Joe Chamberlain	1959	Cannabiere
1852	Stilton	1901	Reminiscence	1960	New Brig
1853	Kingston	1902	Osbech	1961	Utrillo
1854	Grapeshot	1903	Cliftonhall	1962	Bordone
1855	Whitelock	1904	Palmy Days	1963	Horse Radish
1856	Zeta	1905	Princess Florizel	1964	Peter Piper
1857	Underhand	1906	Outbreak	1965	Cagirama
1858	Underhand	1907	Killigrew	1966	Sweet Story
1859	Underhand	1908	Old China	1967	Piaco
1860	First Lord	1909	Sir Harry	1968	Amateur
1861	Joey Jones	1910	Elizabetta	1969	Even Say
1862	Montebello	1911	Pilo	1970	Philoctetes
1863	Caller Ou	1912	Mynora	1971	Tartar Prince
1864	Caller Ou	1913	The Tylt	1972	Scoria
1865	Brown Bread	1914	The Guller	1973	Tom Cribb
1866	Rococo	1919	Trestle	1974	Attivo
1867	Fervacques	1920	Irish Lake	1975	Grey God
1868	Fortunio	1921	Hunt Law	1976	Philominski
1869	The Spy	1922	Double Hackle	1977	Tug of War
1870	Kennington	1923	Carpathus	1978	Tug of War
1871	Taraban	1924	Jazzband	1979	Totowah
1872	Spenithorne	1925	Obliterate	1980	Mons Beau
1873	Falkland	1926	Foxlaw	1981	Dawn Johnny
1874	Lily Agnes	1927	Border Minstrel	1983	Weaver's Pin
1875	Harriet Laws	1928	Primrose League	1984	Karadar
1876	Snail	1929	Ballynahinch	1985	Trade Line
1877	Hampton	1930	Show Girl	1986	Sneak Preview
1878	Glastonbury	1931	Blue Vison	1987	Treasure Hunter
1879	Clearhead	1932	Pomarrel	1988	Stavordale
1880	Micenae	1933	Leonard	1989	Orpheus
1881	Bonnie Doon	1934	Whiteplains	1990	